Opus Est

Six Composers from Northern Europe

From P.B. and Op. &

Paul Rapoport

Opus Est:

Six Composers from Northern Europe

Matthijs Vermeulen, Vagn Holmboe, Havergal Brian,
Allan Pettersson, Fartein Valen, Kaikhosru Shapurji Sorabji

A Crescendo Book
Taplinger Publishing Company, New York

171035

Published in 1979 by Taplinger Publishing Company,
New York.
Copyright © 1978 Paul Rapoport

ISBN 0-8008-5844-1

Printed in Great Britain

Contents

List of Illustrations

Acknowledgements

This book was written while I held an I.W. Killam memorial post-doctoral scholarship at the University of Alberta, Edmonton Alberta Canada. My thanks for making the book possible go to the Killam Scholarship Committee and the Department of Music at that university.

I am grateful to the following individuals and organizations for information and materials of many kinds:

The Concertgebouw Orchestra (Amsterdam), The Donemus Foundation (Amsterdam), The Royal Library (The Hague), Thea Vermeulen-Diepenbrock.

Edition Wilhelm Hansen (Copenhagen), Vagn Holmboe.

Lewis Foreman, Graham Hatton, Malcolm MacDonald (Calum MacDonald), Robert Simpson and Angela Musgrave of the B.B.C. (London), Richard Valéry of Cranz and Co. (London).

Leif Aare, The Baltimore Symphony Orchestra, Rolf Davidson, Nordiska Musikförlaget (Stockholm), Allan Pettersson, The Stockholm Philharmonic Orchestra, The Swedish Institute for National Concerts (Stockholm), The Swedish Music Information Centre (Stockholm), Swedish Radio (Stockholm).

Agnes Hiorth, Else Christie Kielland, Bjarne Kortsen, Harald Lyche and Co. (Drammen), Norsk Musikforlag (Oslo), The Norwegian Music Collection of the University of Oslo Library, Arvid Vollsnes.

Kenneth Derus, Donald Garvelmann, Alistair Hinton, Frank Holliday, Malcolm MacDonald (Calum MacDonald), Kaikhosru Shapurji Sorabji, The University of Cape Town Library.

David Levine, Jon Skinner, Paul Snook, Richard Tiedman.

The music examples are reprinted as follows:

from Matthijs Vermeulen's symphonies nos. 2, 3, 4, 5, and 6 by permission of The Donemus Foundation (Amsterdam).

from Vagn Holmboe's *Epitaph* and Symphony No. 7 by permission of Vagn Holmboe; from his *Monolith* and *Epilog* by permission of Edition Wilhelm Hansen (Copenhagen).

from Havergal Brian's Symphony No. 1, *The Gothic*, by permission of Cranz and Co. (London).

from Allan Pettersson's symphonies nos. 2 and 9 by permission of Allan Pettersson.

from Fartein Valen's *Sonetto di Michelangelo* by permission of Norsk Musikforlag (Oslo) — this work is Copyright 1936 by Norsk Musikforlag A/S, Oslo; from his *Cantico di Ringraziamento, Nenia,* and *An die Hoffnung* by permission of Harald Lyche and Co. (Drammen).

from Kaikhosru Shapurji Sorabji's *Opus Clavicembalisticum* by permission of Kaikhosru Shapurji Sorabji.

The music autograph manuscript pages are reprinted as follows:

from Havergal Brian's Symphony No. 1, *The Gothic*, by permission of Cranz and Co. (London).

from Kaikhosru Shapurji Sorabji's *Opus Clavicembalisticum* by permission of the University of Cape Town Library, where the manuscript has the reference number TPA 781.4.

The photographs are reprinted as follows:

of Matthijs Vermeulen by permission of Thea Vermeulen-Diepenbrock; of Vagn Holmboe by permission of Vagn Holmboe (photo by Davidsen Foto); of Havergal Brian by permission of Lewis Foreman (photo by Lionel Wood); of Allan Pettersson by permission of Nordiska Musikförlaget (photo by Bertil S-son Åberg); of Fartein Valen by permission of Agnes Hiorth; of Kaikhosru Shapurji Sorabji by permission of Frank Holliday (photo by Norman Peterkin).

Paul Rapoport

I Introduction

This book has two chief aims. One is to introduce the work of six composers whose names and music are little known to those most involved with the music of the past seven or eight decades. The other is to question certain assumptions about 20th-century music and its history.

This history is most often dealt with in terms of the works of a limited number of composers and of certain aesthetic, stylistic, or technical concepts or technological discoveries and inventions. One of the better introductory histories, at least for the first half of the century, William Austin's *Music in the 20th Century*, concentrates on Schoenberg, Bartók, Stravinsky, and some jazz musicians, with lesser levels of emphasis on other composers whom Austin considers form various lesser ranks behind this group. Several other books do the same sort of thing, although their choice and ordering of composers may be different. There is nothing wrong with this approach, provided that it is understood to answer questions only from certain perspectives. It is necessary but not sufficient for a detailed understanding of 20th-century music.

One basic question answered by many of these general studies might be put as follows: "Who and what have been the leading composers and concepts in this music?" This is an obvious first question which might be asked by anyone knowing something about music from any era who wants to increase her or his understanding of 20th-century music. The question[1] presupposes at least that what *leading* means is reasonably obvious and that there *are* leading composers and

[1] See footnotes p. 22

concepts. The two presuppositions are not really separate, nor are they as trivial as they might seem.

Leading may imply high quality, which is by no means easily defined. It also implies that a particular composer (or a style, technique, invention, etc.) deserving that adjective has gained some prominence through influence on many others, that some unique achievement has proved to be a fertile resource for further compositional exploration. But *influence* and all that goes with it is not a matter of music alone. Compositions do not beget other compositions. Factors pertaining to artistic influence, inasmuch as they involve products of individual people, may be psychological, sociological, economic, political, etc.[2] What sort of influence might Schoenberg, Bartók, and Stravinsky have had if they had never left Austria, Hungary, and Russia respectively, or if they and many others had not gone to the U.S.A.? What if they had not found congenial publishing arrangements or if gramophone reproduction had been invented somewhat later than it was? What if certain composers had not had the means of dealing with the demands of the musical and nonmusical worlds they were part of? What if there had been no economic depression and no second world war? These are slightly preposterous questions, of course. Their purpose is not to be answered but to suggest that the history of music, especially but not only in the 20th century, is to a large extent the history of its transmission and not just of its composition. This means in turn that we must understand more than we do now of the many things in western-European derived culture (if there indeed still is such an entity) that determine what music is; which kinds of music are heard, studied, and valued in which ways by which groups of people; and how, in light of all this (to return to *influence*), various living traditions are manifested.

Thus, whether composers come to be influences on others may depend on many things other than characteristics or quality of their music *per se*.

There is another set of reasons why the idea of leading composers and concepts may not be as useful as it seems. These reasons involve a proposed inapplicability to 20th-century music of the essence of some historical theories, principally those from the 19th and late 18th centuries which imply that any or all of the following somewhat related statements are true.

1 Each period in music history is dominated by a very few great composers and their styles. All the others are peripheral and unessential for an understanding of the period. (Great Man Theory)
2 Each period is greater than the previous one. Music composition shows a line of qualitative progress through history. (Progress Theory)
3 Musical styles grow out of and replace previous styles and become increasingly complex and differentiated. (Evolution Theory)
4 The music of every period has a group of characteristics imposed upon it by the spirit of the period, its customs, and its ways of thinking. (*Zeitgeist* Theory)

The question of whether these views are useful for the study of pre-20th-century music is interesting but will not be discussed here.[3] For music of approximately the past seven or eight decades, these theories fail, some for different reasons than others, but all of them also for one main reason. They presume a musical culture which on the whole either reveals or seems likely to lead to a fairly consistent, unified, widely shared set of philosophies and procedures. But what philosophical, stylistic, technological, political, or other concerns can be found in common amongst the vast range of musical creations of the recent past? *In common* is a relative term, of course. But in comparison with older music from at least as far back as the renaissance, 20th-century music as a "whole" is clearly much more heterogeneous.[4] Moreover, this heterogeneous and philosophically pluralistic musical scene shows no signs of becoming anything else.[5] For many years there have been composers of tonal, atonal, serial, electronic, and various kinds of indeterminate music, not to mention composers of the many "popular" musics and composers who reject the most basic assumptions about music that have been held implicitly for centuries. We are not in a transitional period in the usual meaning of that phrase, because there is no direction towards anything substantially less pluralistic and diverse.

There have indeed been leading composers and concepts in 20th-century music. But there have been many contemporaneous ones radically different from each other and in various states of independent flux. The importance of determining who and what *the* leading composers and concepts are is reduced, then, and is negligible if one goes about it with false assumptions.

To recapitulate: the notion of leading composers and concepts is of quite reduced importance, because of the apparent stability of a radically new heterogeneous musical culture, and because musical influence depends on many as yet imperfectly understood forces beyond music compositions themselves. This does not mean that influence does not occur or is a useless concept, that originality means nothing, or that all composers are of equal merit. It does mean that influence should be used much less as a criterion of a composer's value. Even if one believes that influence in some way implies greatness, it is an elementary fallacy to conclude that lack of influence implies lack of greatness. Even if influence is in a small way sufficient, it is not therefore necessary. That the six composers discussed in this book (and other composers) have had little influence is no reason why they should continue to be ignored as much as they have been. Nor can a good reason for their continued obscurity be found in the supposition that they are too much influenced by others and have few distinctive ideas or styles of their own — for this is merely untrue. Their best music seems to me skilful, original, profound, and rich in implications for musicians and nonmusicians alike.

If this is so, it is worth asking why they are unknown, for isn't it the *best* music, whatever that means, which is successful, best known, and "survives" the longest? The answer is not "No" but rather the further question "Why should it be?" Music is studied, performed, published, broadcast, and recorded for reasons that may only incidentally relate to the music itself. It is well known, for example, that by far most orchestras play very little recent, unfamiliar, or unusual music. This does not confirm that other music is better. Rather, it reflects, among other things, the fact that older, more familiar, or less unusual music is cheaper to produce

and far more acceptable to basically very conservative direc-
tors, musicians, and audiences. Organizations which run
orchestras, whether labour or management, are social and
financial institutions far more than musical ones.

Artistic value and evaluative judgement have been mentioned several times in this introduction without being defined. I can not define them and I have not seen any other
attempts to do so which are satisfactory, considering the
already discussed great diversity of recently created music.

It is sometimes quite amusing, when it is not infuriating, to
read critical evaluations of music and note how illogical they
are, and when they are more logical, how they presume conditions which do not exist. An example of the latter is the
thousands of outraged negative evaluations of John Cage's
music because it is "not music". As statements of personal
dislike they may be quite interesting and tell us much about
contemporary musical culture. But as rational evaluations
they are worthless. In their extreme but not uncommon forms,
they imply that there is a unique and simple definition of
music to construct and use, that it is universally and eternally
correct, and that it is the *sine qua non* of meaningful aesthetic
experience of aural stimuli. It is equally ludicrous, of course,
that devotees of Cage's music or any other, whether of the
socalled avant-garde or not, should argue for the permanent,
ubiquitous irrelevance of, for example, Beethoven.

Quite often, *composers* dismiss other composers (living or
dead) in an illogical way. But in so doing they are really pro-
tecting their own creativity, which has little in common with
logical discourse but which they might feel is threatened by it.
After all, if composer X admits great value in composer Y's
music, then there is always the "logical" question, "Why
doesn't composer X write like composer Y?" But critics and
other listeners, including performers, and composers who are
able to do so, ought to see and avoid the trap. There is no
reason why individuals can not enjoy, understand, and learn
from musics of widely differing natures and conflicting
philosophies. The three composers discussed in this book
who are alive (and the relatives and associates of the other
three) might be surprised or annoyed to find that an admirer
of the music dealt with in the book is also an admirer of John

Cage's music, but there is nothing illogical or wrong with wide tastes, particularly for performers, researchers, and teachers. Too many critics act as if value of one music denies the possibility of value to a quite different music, and moreover that firm and exclusive evaluative judgement should be the prime goal of musical experience. The very complex matter of evaluative criticism of compositions is but one aspect of musical experience and research, and by no means always separable from other aspects or always open to logical discussion.

Values are of course not purely subjective and personal; they can be discussed profitably from many points of view. But highly reasoned comparison and evaluation of the six composers and their works is not one of this book's aims. It is hoped, rather, that the discussion of these composers' lives and music will lead those interested to examine them for themselves and come to their own conclusions consistent, or perhaps better yet, inconsistent with their own thinking on other musical matters. Certainly the inclusion of these composers in the book implies that I think they should be valued highly. They provide musical experiences to receptive listeners which can not be found in music by other composers, however well known or influential they have been. This is too difficult to *prove* in words: linguistic discourse and musical discourse are too much mismatched. But in the course of the whole book I think that it will be suggested very strongly.

The six composers were born between 1876 and 1911 and were active[6] from just before 1900 to the present. All six lived and worked in northern Europe: two in England, one each in the Netherlands, Denmark, Sweden, and Norway. The historical, political, and economic reasons for the assigning of "periphery" status to these countries in musical matters have affected the potentiality of their composers for becoming known internationally.

The language barrier is another restricting factor for the Scandinavian and Dutch composers: *somewhat* restricting for the mere transmission of the music to the English-speaking world, and certainly more so for a fuller understanding of it. Cultural transmission is simply easier between individuals or countries speaking the same language, and those speaking and reading only one language can not, of course, conduct much research on foreign music. Thus, the fact that Dutch and the Scandinavian languages are much less known in the English-speaking world than, for example, French and German, is a further hindrance to widespread knowledge about these composers.

In addition to being approximate contemporaries and from the less influential area of northern Europe, the six composers all wrote music for nonelectronic instruments in a standard five-line staff notation. Their music retains at least some traces of tonality and assumes standard, essentially 19th-century ideas about the roles of and the relationships among composer, performer, and listener. All six also wrote at least a few works titled *Symphony*. They are "traditionalists", then, but this label does not mean that their music is conventional, reactionary, and irrelevant, or is to be marked neoclassical, neoromantic, or neo- something else and popped away into a neatly compartmentalized filing cabinet of musical "isms". Categorization, like evaluation, has its uses in music, but if it is treated as an end of musical understanding instead of a means to it, then the variety, subtlety, and individuality of the music is ignored and categorization does more harm than good. The person who automatically dismisses music by composers who write symphonies[7] makes a mistake of just this kind.

The chapters on the individual composers are not surveys of their works, although general characteristics of them are often brought into the discussion. Musical surveys have their place, and good ones, leading to meaningful syntheses of a large amount of material, are always necessary. But they are not the only means of introducing composers. In this book the opposite approach has been chosen, namely to concentrate on one or a few major works by each composer. Perhaps more appetites will be whetted this way; certainly a more focussed discussion is made possible. Furthermore, since the music will be unknown to most people, a survey here would be somewhat bewildering to follow, especially as most of the important compositions of the approximately 700 by the six composers are difficult to find, as either scores or records. Any extensive survey is useful only if the generalizations made can be repeatedly substantiated by reference to the music and other documents. The limited availability of the large amount of music which might be discussed here means that sufficient references would have to be included in the book, making it enormous and virtually unreadable. The only other alternative would be superficiality.

Implicit in this reasoning is the principle that nothing should be taken for granted. If people knew how poorly a great deal of research is carried out and reported on, they would stop believing so much of what they read. If one is seriously interested in a subject, one should investigate as many independent sources on it as possible. Even the best researchers, writers, editors, and printers make mistakes in relatively simple matters. And when it comes to complex conclusions from complex data, the thinking reader is always suspicious rather than trusting.

Of the nine compositions dealt with in some detail in this book, one is published but not recorded, one is recorded but not published, and seven are both published and recorded. There are serious faults in some of these scores and records. But those who wish to can track down these materials plus many other bibliographic items and judge for themselves: not only to verify that part of what is written in this book which is verifiable, but also, as has been pointed out, to explore the lives and music of these composers in their own ways.

No defence should be needed for the "life and music" approach which the following six chapters take. Certainly insofar as all the composers may be considered western Europeans, their music can be heard, studied, and compared with little reference to their lives. But natural questions like "What sort of person wrote this music?" are not idle. They lead to further questions about 20th-century musical creativity and its relation to, for example, politics, old age, criticism, and professional obscurity. While the six chapters do not take up these matters in detail, they do provide, chiefly through the biographical portions, information for further enquiries in these areas.

The book will, I hope, make another contribution — although it will be only a marginal one — to the history of symphonic composition in western music. There has been some discussion elsewhere of what the *compositional* term *symphonic* means (especially in relation to orchestral music, to which it is most frequently applied), as opposed to the *title-label symphony*,[8] which may or may not designate a composition whose content, form, style, techniques, procedures, etc. are really symphonic, i.e. compositionally symphonic. All the fairly recent definitions I have seen of *compositionally symphonic*, while having good properties, either are too vague or make unsubstantiated assumptions, for example about the necessity of the form pattern known as sonata, or of tonality.[9] Someday someone may improve on these definitions and tackle the relationship between the title-label and the compositional term in the past two and a half centuries. Whoever does it will not, I trust, ignore 20th-century northern Europe or the music of these six composers. Altogether they have used the title-label *symphony* or its adjective *symphonic* about 100 times.

Eight of the individual works focussed on are indeed orchestral. Five of the six composers were indeed chosen because they wrote a large number of orchestral works or because a large part of what reputation they have is based on those works.[10] Many problems of their obscurity, and hence many of the issues raised in this chapter, relate to this emphasis on orchestral music.[11]

The exception in this, as in so many other matters, is Kaikhosru Shapurji Sorabji. He has written orchestral music, but none of it has ever been performed, for reasons which will become clear. Partly because of this, but mainly because most of his works are for solo piano, it is a solo piano composition which is discussed in detail in the chapter devoted to him. His piano music is as "orchestral" as any, so there is even a certain appropriateness to his inclusion in a book primarily about orchestral composers. Sorabji is also from the only country (England) to have two composers in this book. But the emphasis remains on six different individuals, not the music of five different countries.

Four of the six composers wrote substantial amounts of music criticism. Little of this non-English material has been translated. Little of any of it is easily found, because most of it appeared originally in newspapers or journals, or books which have long been out of print. The following chapters

contain excerpts from the composers' own writings, which
should provide a clearer picture of their work as a whole.
Their opinions at certain times in their careers are often well
represented by their own words and in prose styles which
often bear striking resemblance to their musical styles. But
by no means is everything they write true, nor are the implications of their writing only what the authors thought they
were. Many people believe that what composers write, especially about themselves, is the first and last word on something,
but often their writing must be taken at more or less than face
value. In the following chapters there is little direct comment
on this problem, but the quotations and bibliographical references will point to a great deal of primary material to explore.
All the translations in the book, of these quotations and of
other material, are my own unless there is a note stating
otherwise.

Each chapter first presents biographical material and then
musical analysis. The analysis is concerned chiefly with style
and form in broad senses. The approaches to both parts of the
chapters are different in each case and depend partly on what
has already been written elsewhere about these composers.
For example: a few years ago there was not much information
available about Havergal Brian's life and music, but recently
four books have appeared about him.[12] Thus, the chapter
here on Brian does not repeat what is to be found in those
books. The biographical part is a review of them, a guide for
those who might wish to read them. The analytical part concerns one of Brian's works that has been written about before
at some length, but here it is treated from a completely new
viewpoint.

Fartein Valen is the only other composer who has been the
subject of fairly large published biographies. But unlike the
recent biographies of Brian, one of those about Valen is hard
to find and the other is written in Norwegian. Thus, the biographical part of the chapter about him is more straightforward than the one about Brian. Four short works of Valen's
are the subject of the analytical part. The analysis there, unlike that in the other chapters, is contrastive and is directed
towards removing some of the existing confusion about the
order of composition of the works in question.

At the end of each chapter there is a chronological list of the composer's main works involving orchestra, which for reasons of space omits concertos for specific instruments, operas, other stage works, incidental music, songs, works which were never finished, and any works totally lost or destroyed which were never performed. Works for string orchestra are included. (None of these composers wrote anything still extant for band or other nonchamber wind ensemble.) For Sorabji, the main works for solo piano are given instead.

This basic list of a composer's works includes titles, subtitles, opus numbers, dates of composition, and information on first performances and published scores. An asterisk (*) designates a work at least part of which has been commercially recorded. Titles of works are unofficial; composers sometimes give a work different titles, even on the same manuscript. Names of orchestras are also unofficial; many of these are translations and may not match the official translated title if there is one.

This list is followed by brief mention of works in other categories, a discography, a note on location of autograph music manuscripts, and a selective bibliography divided into writings by the composer and writings by others about the composer.

The discography is chronological by date of composition of the works recorded. All records are twelve-inch stereo unless otherwise noted. The performers listed for a specific work are not necessarily the same for other works on the same record.

The bibliographies of writings are chronological by date of publication of the articles and books listed. Inclusion of items in these various lists does not imply approval of them.

Appendix I at the end of the book lists the forces required to perform the orchestral works discussed in detail in chapters II to VI. Appendix II provides further information made available between the time the book was completed and just before press time.

The references under the music examples are to the published versions mentioned in the basic lists of works. A few slight errors in the published scores have been corrected without comment. The page references in the Vermeulen examples (Chapter II), except for those from his fourth symphony, are to the numbers at the *bottom* of the pages of the published scores. The Pettersson examples (Chapter V) are from unpublished works. The copies used were borrowed from S.T.I.M. (Stockholm): item no. 428 for Pettersson's Symphony No. 2, and no. 1395/2 for his Symphony No. 9. Both were photocopies of Pettersson's autograph manuscripts.

In the music examples, all the abbreviations for instruments and voices have three letters:

bct	bass clarinet	sax	saxophone
bel	bell	sbs	string bass
brs	brass	scm	suspended cymbal
bsn	bassoon	sdr	side drum
cbn	contrabassoon	sop	soprano
cel	celesta	spn	sopranino
clo	cello	str	string
clt	clarinet	tam	tamtam
Ehn	English horn	tba	tuba
flt	flute	tbn	trombone
hrn	horn	tpt	trumpet
hrp	harp	vib	vibraphone
obo	oboe	vla	viola
orc	orchestra	vln	violin
pic	piccolo	wnd	wind
prc	percussion	wwd	woodwind
		xyl	xylophone

Plurals have *s* added. For specified wind instruments (woodwinds and brass), plurals imply the number 2 unless another number appears (e.g. "hrns" vs. "4 hrns"). The following additional abbreviations appear in the lists of works:

1st prf	first performance
Pbd	published
cdr.	conductor
P.O.	Philharmonic Orchestra
S.O.	Symphony Orchestra

In the music examples, Î means *sounding an octave higher* Į *sounding an octave lower*, ÎÎ *sounding two octaves higher* etc. (Otherwise, all lines are written at sounding pitch.) The cancellation for these signs is a written lower-case l, standing for *loco*.

In the instrumental indications in the examples, the octave transposition signs do not apply across commas. Thus "clos, sbss ɭ" means *cellos, and string basses sounding an octave lower*, not *cellos and string basses (both) sounding an octave lower*. The symbols + and - used with instrument names denote additions and subtractions to the texture respectively. Thus *+vlas* at a certain point would imply violas are added to the forces already playing a certain line, *-vlas* that they stop playing that line there. In the examples, *all* the notes or instruments in any whole original passage may not be given. For music played by string and other instruments together, the slur marks given are most often those of the non-string instrument(s).

The only terms used in the book which may need clarification are *pitch class* and *interval class*. *Pitch* by itself refers to a tone in a specific location, e.g. contra-A^b or C-256. *Pitch class* refers to any or all of the tones having the same name. Thus a composition in the key of D would emphasize the pitch class D; which *pitches* named D it emphasized would be unknown before it was seen or heard.

An *interval* is, of course, the undirected distance between two pitches. An *interval class* in this book refers to the set of intervals which reduce to the same interval solely by means of octave transposition. The intervals of a minor second, major seventh, and minor ninth are thus all members of the *interval class* called *minor second*; the intervals of a fourth, fifth, eleventh, and twelfth are all members of the *interval class* called *fourth*. For convenience, there are no interval classes larger than half an octave, commonly called *tritone*, *augmented fourth*, or *diminished fifth*. Sometimes the context of a discussion makes the exact usage of these terms unnecessary, but often the exact distinctions are important.

Footnotes to Chapter I

1   Other wordings of similar questions would lead to the same general results as are presented here.

2   None of these ideas is new. See especially Alan Merriam: *The Anthropology of Music* ([Evanston, Illinois, U.S.A.:] Northwestern University Press, 1964).

3   See especially Warren Dwight Allen: *Philosophies of Music History — A Study of General Histories of Music 1600-1960* (New York: Dover, 1962). Some views Allen presents have been modified here.

4   Of course, one could divide the 20th century into subperiods, but doing so would not affect the basic argument presented here.

5   This idea is also not new. See especially Chapters 8 and 9 in Leonard Meyer: *Music, the Arts, and Ideas* (Chicago: University of Chicago Press, 1967). Since Meyer's book was written, the "musical scene" has become a little less pluralistic, less wild, and less radically politicized. But even if it is less heterogeneous than it was in the mid-1960's, there are no signs of a return to the relative homogeneity of, for example, the 19th century.

6   In summary statements such as this, the past tense will be used, even though three of the composers are still living.

7   assuming it is known what a symphony is — see below and Chapter VIII on this subject.

8   or the adjective *symphonic* when it essentially means only "for orchestra".

9   A few further general comments about *compositionally symphonic* will be found in Chapter VIII.

10 As implied earlier, they were also chosen because they are relatively unknown 20th-century composers of a "traditional" type and from different northern European countries.

11 Further discussion of this point will be found in Chapter VIII.

12 Brian is still a relatively unknown composer. With only one major exception, his orchestral music has still not been performed outside Britain.

Matthijs Vermeulen in 1921

II Matthijs Vermeulen and his Symphony No. 2, *Prélude à la Nouvelle Journée*

. . . to arouse and fan the secret fire, le feu sacré, the divine spark which exists in every person, more or less lies imprisoned as things are, and longs to be freed. [1]

In 1930, an article appeared in Holland about Matthijs Vermeulen which spoke of him as "already a legendary figure",[2] "legendary" partly because of his physical remoteness from the Dutch musical scene. At that time he was living near Paris, writing articles mostly on nonmusical topics for an Indonesian paper. A few people knew some of his songs and chamber music, but his three symphonies had not been played, except for a "performance" of one which was really only a preliminary reading through.

The legend was built not so much around his music as around his music criticism, especially of the period 1909-20, when he had been living in Holland. He was a brilliant and volatile writer whose persistent and pugnacious attacks on the Dutch musical establishment gained him few friends and many enemies.

He was an impetuous and naive person in certain ways — even by his own admission — but these traits were balanced by energetic self-confidence and constant pursuit of what he felt was good and true. He was born in Helmond, Holland on 8 February 1888; at the age of 13 he decided to become a composer, and at 18 he set off for Amsterdam with practically no money or experience to realize this unrealistic ambition.

Although his finances and background were insufficient for formal entry into the Amsterdam conservatory, the director, Daniël de Lange, must have found him promising: he gave

[1] See footnotes p. 39

him free lessons in theory and composition on and off for three years (1907-10). In 1910 Vermeulen met the Dutch composer Alphons Diepenbrock, from whom he learned a great deal, although more as a sympathetic younger friend than as a formal student. In composition, Vermeulen was basically self-taught. As a youth he read through whatever music textbooks and scores he could find. Diepenbrock introduced him to the work of various contemporary composers, which he then pursued on his own.

Around 1909 he became a reviewer of the concerts of the Amsterdam Concertgebouw Orchestra, whose conductor since 1895 had been Willem Mengelberg. Vermeulen admired his conducting and organizing abilities and his tireless energies for building up Dutch musical life. But he considered it his moral duty not only to laud but to castigate if necessary. Mengelberg had firm control over several Dutch musical organizations; Vermeulen came to see this as pure dictatorship, with no possibility for competition or even disagreement with Mengelberg's somewhat limited, definitely pro-German tastes. Mengelberg and his followers tried to ignore Vermeulen as much as possible but became angrier as Vermeulen's public criticism continued.

In 1915 or 1916, Vermeulen had the naive audacity to offer his recently completed first symphony to Mengelberg for performance with the Concertgebouw, reasoning that no other performers would do it justice. Mengelberg immediately sent for him, told him what he thought of his criticism, flipped through the score of the symphony, and advised him to take composition lessons with his assistant conductor, Cornelis Dopper. News of this meeting spread. In the following years, it was said that Vermeulen wrote unfavourably about Mengelberg primarily because Mengelberg had refused to play his music, and that Mengelberg had been kind in refusing because he wanted to spare the composer the embarrassment of a performance of his "incompetent" work. Of course, Vermeulen had been criticizing Mengelberg for some time before all this, and it seems unlikely that Mengelberg really understood the symphony.

Vermeulen, determined to sustain his honour as a composer, had the symphony played in 1919 by a provincial orchestra.

Reactions were negative. Two years later, Vermeulen explained why:

> The work was played at the performance with six first, six second violins, four violas (among these fourteen, several were virtually incompetent) [,] two (!!) violoncellos, three (!) contrabasses, one harp. Moreover, it was played from *uncorrected* parts, in which the conductor, through unforgivable slovenliness, had allowed 131 (one hundred thirty-one) errors to go unrectified.[3]

A glance at the symphony or the list of forces required shows that it is no chamber symphony. Possibly the influenza epidemic of the time was responsible for the reduced number of players. In any case, the inadequacy of the playing received almost no mention by the critics. Vermeulen considered that he never really heard the work until it was played again, in 1964.

In recommending Dopper as an example, Mengelberg must have known he would not be taken seriously. For several years Vermeulen had been knocking down Dopper's works, calling them badly eclectic, haphazard, parodistic, and lacking in everything he considered necessary in music. In 1916, on mentioning two symphonic studies by Dopper titled *Paean*, he offered the opinion that Dopper could no more write a true paean than "a completely undisturbed aboriginal of the most remote Thule of the Patagonians" could write a Roman Catholic Credo.[4] Nor was his abuse confined to Dopper. With Dopper, Bernard Zweers, and others in mind, he asked

> Would there be a country where more vegetative dilettantism is cultivated than in the Netherlands? . . . Would there be one country where mediocrity is brought up with so much ardour, and where everything seems set up especially to generate nothing but mediocrity?[5]

Because Mengelberg supported these people in various ways, the shots Vermeulen fired at them he also fired at Mengelberg.

The whole Dopper matter came to a crisis when, in April 1918, after Mengelberg's performance with the Concertgebouw of a work by Dopper, Vermeulen shouted out (probably in his most ironic manner) something like "Down with Dopper, long live Sousa!" The police removed him from the hall, and the Concertgebouw banned him from attending their performances. Years later it was said that soon after this incident he had been fired from his editorial and reviewing position with *De Telegraaf* and had been forced into exile. Actually, the Concertgebouw reinstated him in 1919, and he resigned from the newspaper in 1920, over two years after the shouting incident. Perhaps he resigned because of pressure from his opponents, but he also did so because he felt driven to composition, with which his activities as a critic were interfering. Only in the summer of 1921 did he leave Holland, after the death of Diepenbrock and after his last attempt to have his music played there.

This attempt took the form of three letters written to Mengelberg in April 1921. Vermeulen offered him the second symphony and the first again. By this time, however, he must have known that Mengelberg would have nothing to do with him. The three letters were full of self-satisfaction and taunting sarcasm, which could hardly have been designed to elicit friendliness from the addressee:

> It would really be supremely ironic if I offered this second symphony, which presents such unusual and extraordinary difficulties — difficulties which can be overcome only through total devotion — for interpretation by someone who was not above all an artist.
>
> On the contrary. You yourself have said: "I am above all an artist." (*N[ieuwe] R[otterdamsche] C[ouran]t* 8 Apr.) I am making an appeal, although prematurely, to this autobiographical résumé.[6]

Mengelberg did not reply. Vermeulen published the letters, but there was no significant reaction from anyone. He decided to move to France: he had always been a strong Francophile and thought that his chances as a composer were better there than in Holland, where they were now virtually nonexistent. But in the next two decades he had no real success, despite having shown his work to Gabriel Pierné, Walter Straram, Serge Koussevitzky, Pierre Monteux, Leopold Stokowski, and other conductors.

In 1930 there was a performance in Leiden of his incidental music for chorus, speaker, and orchestra, recently commissioned and written to accompany Martinus Nijhoff's *De Vlie-*

gende Hollander. Vermeulen's music had to be recorded on discs to be played back during the outdoor production. Various reports state that high winds rendered nearly inaudible the distorted amplification of the poorly recorded sound.

It was thus not until 1939 that anyone had a good chance to hear his orchestral music properly played. A committee called *Maneto* (acronym for *Manifestatie Nederlandsche Toonkunst*) had been formed, to present concerts of contemporary Dutch music. Vermeulen, still living in France, was asked to send in something for consideration. He sent in all three symphonies he had written. The third was chosen, for performance by Eduard van Beinum and the Concertgebouw. Friends arranged for Vermeulen to give a talk on criticism: with the funds from that, he was able to go to Amsterdam to hear the symphony. He was 51.

Early in the second world war, his work for the Indonesian paper stopped, leaving him with almost no income. Later in the war his wife Annie van Hengst and his oldest son Josquin died. Despite all the difficulties of those years, he was able to complete his two largest works, symphonies 4 and 5. With indomitable faith and optimism he gave the fourth the title *Les Victoires*, having in mind "the countless victories of those who had to achieve victory",[7] and the fifth the title *Les Lendemains Chantants*, "to try, in the midst of the darkness, to relate through music something of the singing tomorrows of a happy future".[8]

In 1946 he returned to Holland and married Diepenbrock's daughter Thea. From 1947 to 1956 he wrote for *De Groene Amsterdammer*; in that decade he also had two books published and had his fourth, fifth, and second symphonies performed for the first time. There may have been resistance in 1949 by Mengelberg supporters in the Concertgebouw to performing the fifth, but at that time Mengelberg was nearly 80 and living in Switzerland, having been banned from carrying out professional musical activities in Holland because of his pro-Nazi position during the war. Vermeulen had the last laugh, if it could be called that.

Finally, in 1956 Vermeulen quit the regular writing of criticism to devote himself full-time to composing — something he had wanted to do for at least 40 years. In 1963, a 75th-birthday concert of his chamber music was produced, but during the last decade of his life, outstanding performances of his orchestral music were still rare. The one major performance outside Holland (in Cologne in 1960) raised little interest. After a long illness, he died on 26 July 1967, still at odds with many people and feeling that he needed still more time to fulfill his intentions.

Vermeulen held very specific views about contemporary music's proper content and function, which he believed he alone was supplying and fulfilling, continuing what had been started by Mahler, Debussy, Ravel, Schoenberg, and a few others. It is perhaps easier to understand what he cherished most in music by considering first what he disliked most: neoclassicism. In its worst manifestations he found it cold, dull, and cerebral, totally lacking in emotion and in any sense of magical exaltation. He thought that the worst nonsense ever uttered about music was that it could mean nothing at all. He probably realized that Stravinsky and others who said this at various times were exaggerating in order to sweep away what they found to be the excesses of romanticism, particularly in its Wagnerian and Straussian varieties. But on occasion he took Stravinsky literally, found a meaninglessness in his and others' music regardless of any stated doctrine, and berated them roundly for it. To him the greatest waste for a composer was to leave listeners unmoved, through some soulless playing with notes, or to attack them through sarcastic or grotesque music.

One may begin to grasp his aims in composition from the titles of his symphonies.[9] They are positive and refer to the future. He believed that his music could release listeners from the ills of the present, and therefore orient them to the future, not so much because he knew details of the future, but because he had faith that it had to be better spiritually than the present. His concerns were beauty, joy, and love, and how to lead and be led by them through music. These were familiar concerns, of course, and he readily acknowledged that. But he traced them far beyond the 19th century, from which they can easily be perceived to have come, to the 14th and 15th centuries, and ultimately to what he imagined as the beginning of music, when humanity first began to sing and to con-

ribute to and reveal the essence of what he called the fundamental "creator spirit" of the universe. On an only slightly
less metaphysical level, he once wrote, quoting Diepenbrock,
that music was "the sensation of the force that sets things in
motion, 'the love' that drives the sun and the other stars".[10]
In all his music he strove to capture and release something of
his sensation.

His most significant writings are full of the same independ-
ence and strong emotion that his music is, and the same mystical reflection and revelation that might also be heard in his
music. There are many things to disagree with in his writings,
but they make a lively contribution towards a better understanding of his music and towards a rethinking of fundamental issues in other music, whether or not one comes to the
same conclusions as he did about them. It is refreshing, for
example, to read his objections to a lot of German music long
considered great, and his making a case for medieval and renaissance music, which today is still heard far less often than
it should be. A study of the relation between Vermeulen's
writings and his music would also be interesting from the
viewpoints of style and creativity in their broadest senses. He
became a writer chiefly to make a living, but his articles and
books reveal important parts of him that had to be communicated in words when they could not be communicated in
music.

Vermeulen had no use for well-known form patterns such
as sonata, fugue, and rondo, because they were based on principles of repetition and duality, such as tonal, thematic, and
motivic conflict. For him these ideas involved music of too
restricted a type and were out of date, no longer able "to answer to the desires, conscious or unconscious, of our inner
being".[11] He was interested in something freer, in which the
musical action might not be controlled by any fixed groupings
of instruments or any one, fixed metric scheme, tonality, or
melody. The basis of his style is a polymelody in which nearly
all the individual lines are equal, each going its own way, sup-
porting the others but only indirectly and opaquely. The result of this, he believed, would bring forth a new kind of ex-
hilarating release in music — new at least since the 17th century — music in which "the centre of gravity and the strictures

of gravitational force entailed by it may be eliminated and the sensation given of freedom in time and space".[12]

The analogy to physics was deliberate, as was the analogy to social psychology when Vermeulen wrote that in listening to a symphony by any true composer, "quite quickly we lose the notion of our personal identity . . . We are transformed into a human mixture and each of us becomes multitude."[13] The sociopolitical implications are even clearer in the following:

> There are in this future orchestra, in this music, no pre-eminences, no ranks. There is a community, which works to obtain a harmonious result, but each member of the collectivity works in his own way, according to his own nature, his own insight. Each one represents his entire self in the orchestral, musical unanimity, his whole ego, with all his opportunities unimpeded, unconfined. Towards the combined undertaking, each contributes as a total person, with full heart and soul, with all his abilities. Each is first cause, first impulse. Each is also tendency and endpoint. Each sings his own essence, his own role, his own melody, his own rhythm. Each is free. Each is equal. Although each serves, none is subservient. Each sings his own music, which in the group action becomes the music of all. And just as the old orchestra was the projection of a former society, human being, and state, so shall this evolved orchestra be the projection of a new earth to be realized.[14]

The implied starting point in Vermeulen's mind was melody, which he felt had been shunned by composers after the first world war. He said that if melody were to dominate as the essential and basic representative of motion and life, music had to go back at least to the period before the vertical, or tonal polyphony of the baroque, to the renaissance and the middle ages. The idea of *cantus firmus* is in fact the structural basis of his symphonies. For Vermeulen, this meant a melody which undergoes considerable and possibly unpredictable changes because it both governs the action of the music and evolves with it. The other lines of the music are in theory and frequently in practice of similar construction and equal importance. Thus it is often difficult and at times actually unimportant to trace the course of a particular *cantus firmus* in one work, especially as the *cantus firmus* is not always present, any more than it had to be in, say, a 15th-century *cantus firmus* mass.

Although Vermeulen's seven symphonies span more than 50 years, they have much in common as a group of works. They all play without pause except for no. 5, and even in that symphony the pauses do not separate sharply differing movements. In each symphony, polymelodic constructions are often emphasized by very distinct tone colours of nonstandard instruments (e.g. saxophones, soprano clarinets, or soprano trumpets in E^b). Simple ostinatos are also used, sometimes with a definitely military sound, as rhythmic, harmonic, and/ or timbral backgrounds for other activities. Sometimes they impart an effect of severity and of restless exuberance (see ex. 1) not unlike tendencies observable in the composer's own character.

Nearly all the symphonies have several climactic passages which, although comprising only four or five independent lines, are extraordinarily free and wild. Ostinatos do not figure as prominently in these passages, but these passages do make occasional use of canon. The canons often give an impression of real frenzy, of two or more lines vigorously chasing each other.

The melodies themselves are often chromatic and emphasize interval classes of seconds and fourths, notably semitones and tritones. Many of the melodies are aperiodic, have a limited range, and tend to fold back into themselves. Their surface rhythmic freedom is often achieved by the irregular sequence of what is really a limited number of basic rhythms (see ex. 2) and their dotted variants. All these attributes contribute to the melodies' lyrical restlessness. Exs. 3 to 6, from four separate works, illustrate these several points.

According to the score, Vermeulen began his Symphony No. 2, *Prélude à la Nouvelle Journée*, on 4 June 1919 and finished it on 3 December 1920. As mentioned earlier, he suggested to Mengelberg in 1921 that Mengelberg perform it with the Concertgebouw Orchestra. Despite this and other attempts at having it heard, the symphony lay unperformed until 1953. Many Dutch sources say the first performance was on 5 July 1956 in Amsterdam, but the symphony was played first (and probably broadcast live) on 9 December 1953 in Brussels. Vermeulen had sent it in to the 1953 international competition in composition in the name of Queen Elisabeth

of Belgium. From the 439 works submitted, a jury had to eli-
minate all but twelve in a very short time. Then a second jury
had to vote on the final ranking of those twelve after hearing
them each played once by Franz André and one of two
Belgian orchestras, in public performances which in some
cases were probably inadequate. Vermeulen's symphony was
placed fifth and won him the prize of the city of Brussels, a
silver medal and 50,000 French francs. Because he did not
hear the Belgian performance, he first heard the symphony in
its first Dutch performance, nearly 36 years after he wrote it.

The symphony is full of sharp, strident lines like ex. 7,
which gives the first occurrence of the main theme, vividly
proclaimed by eleven wind instruments. It is heard over an
irregularly thumping string and percussion ostinato built on
the chord of ex. 8. The initial leaps up in ex. 7 are characteristic of the theme in many of its otherwise quite altered returns. The leaps undergo certain immediate changes themselves, as is shown in ex. 9, which covers only 15 measures of
music. But still prevalent are interval classes of the tritone
and the second (major and minor). Equally important are the
semitones separating the notes marked X and those marked Y.
The larger-level restricted motion so outlined produces an
overall *suspension* of melodic activity, against which is heard
the more lively foreground of the melody.

In fuller textures, a sense of immobility may also be present,
aided by the polytonality and atonality of the combination
of freely moving lines. Often there are no dominant-tonic relations, no *one* "gravitational" relationship in the harmonies,
and no simple rhythmic patterns that produce even potential
points of agreement among the individual lines. The lines by
themselves may contain many tonal implications, but when
heard simultaneously, these implications do not support each
other, nor do the lines remain polytonally distinct. Thus, a
kind of atonality results.

The most striking places in Vermeulen's symphonies that
illustrate this are those wild climaxes referred to earlier. The
wildest one in the second symphony goes from fig. 23 to fig.
28 in the score (ex. 10 is an extract of this) at the end of the
third of the work's five main sections. Single lines have their
own identity and there is only one measured tempo, but the

ebullient, orgiastic polyphony as a unit has no reference to what is normally called tonality. Here, then, Vermeulen a-chieves a radical realization of his ideals of independent mo-tion and ecstatic release from physical limitations. The effect is truly overwhelming.

Even though the symphony is partly atonal, it can also be heard as being in a key of C. Sections may be perceived as keyless on their own but at least as marginally tonal when considered on the larger level of the relationships among whole sections. There are certain patterns of prominent pitches which emerge only when sections are indeed con-sidered as divisions of something larger, as the following dis-cussion illustrates.

The sustained final sound of the symphony is a full orches-tration of the chord in ex. 11 (again, it is comprised mainly of interval classes of seconds and fourths). Throughout the composition, the pitches of the chord are emphasized in struc-turally significant ways in ostinatos, melodic lines, longer passages, sections, etc. One of the first instances of this em-phasis is contained in ex. 7. Its first two measures are nothing but G, C# or Db, and F, and these pitch classes remain im-portant throughout the example. The C that is "missing" al-together in ex. 7 is in fact the root of ex. 8, the seven-note chord sounded by the "irregularly thumping string and per-cussion ostinato" mentioned earlier as accompanying ex. 7.

The tonal relationships set up by ex. 7 and its accompani-ment develop over long stretches of time. For this reason, they are difficult to grasp, but once grasped, they are very striking. The final chord then becomes almost as "logical" as any final chord might be in classical tonality.

Vermeulen described his second symphony in the pro-gramme note for the first Dutch performance as being in five sections. This description is accurate as far as it goes and im-plies the following:

Section 1 : beginning to fig. 9 (p. 19)
Section 2 : fig. 9 to fig. 12 (p. 25)
Section 3 : fig. 12 to fig. 28 (p. 61)
Section 4 : fig. 28 to fig. 37 (p. 81)
Section 5 : fig. 37 to end

Section 1 is concerned chiefly with the establishment of the main theme, sounding it in different shapes over various accompaniments, some very active, others less so, but all of them contributing to a marked tension. This section contains a long, piercing line for four piccolos and first violins (ex. 12). It may seem merely a sharply obtrusive addition to the texture, but it is much more. In section 3, when an oboe and then a piccolo sustain just their high F (*pp*, in quiet, thin textures), they instantly echo the part of section 1 which ex. 12 comes from. They do this as much by repetition of range and timbre as by pitch itself. In Vermeulen's symphonies, range and particularly timbre can be almost as important thematically as any melodic shape or rhythm.

Sections 2 and 3 increase the activity gradually. Ostinato backgrounds are again frequent and are familiar in the intervals they contain (see ex. 13). At one point a beautiful, slow moving, chant-like melody, spread over six octaves in piccolo flutes, harps, and muted strings is heard together with faster moving varied fragments of the main theme in parallel root position triads in the woodwinds and brass (ex. 14). This passage gives the impression of a lucid dream in which two entirely different worlds are coexisting. Section 3 closes with the brilliant climax referred to earlier, a remarkable example of cacophonous concord, music of much action and drama but no conflict or struggle.

Section 4 is mostly quiet and contemplative. Previous ideas are developed, but not dramatically in a motivic sense. Most of the lines are long. New instrumental combinations are heard: English horn, harp, and solo violin; four flutes and bass clarinet four octaves apart over muted strings. Almost always the woodwind and brass instruments are treated in such a way that even when combined they retain their own distinct sound.

Section 5 opens with a new theme (ex. 15, with semitone ascent at the X's) which, like others introduced in this section, undergoes many changes. A very short ostinato first heard in section 4 reappears in the prominent melody whose beginning is ex. 16, in one of the symphony's very few warm mellow moments. The tempo changes frequently in section 5 overall it increases as more lines and instruments are added t the action. The final part, marked *lumineux et éclatant*, completes the gradual reintroduction of transformed versions of the main theme, combining them with many other themes in a dithyrambic fervour. The sound is vehement, even militant, lending an obsessive ferocity to the symphony's conclusion.

Both the opening and closing sections of the second symphony owe something to equivalent places in Beethoven's ninth symphony, which Vermeulen admired greatly. The main theme itself in the second symphony also bears a striking resemblance out of context to the main theme in Skryabin's *Poème de l'Extase*. Vermeulen knew Skryabin's works and was impressed by some of their aims, if not their methods. More generally, Vermeulen's philosophical ideas bear only a little resemblance to things found in Skryabin's mystical theosophy. Vermeulen's musical romanticism also has almost nothing to do with Wagner and Wagner-influenced late 19th-century French music, both of which meant much more to Skryabin.

Vermeulen had a little more affinity with the 19th-century American transcendental philosophers and Charles Ives, although he may not have known the former and almost certainly did not know the latter, at least in 1920. He shared their deep humanism and their concern with the free and immediate experience, the clear and direct revelation of spiritual truths — even though his ideas about realizing in music what he considered these truths to be differed in many ways from Ives'. Vermeulen was also more involved with questions of psychological history and cosmic order, often from religious and specifically European, Catholic-mystical perspectives, whether overt or not. These differences relate very much to Vermeulen's music being less wideranging, eclectic, and irreverent than Ives', and less bizarre in technical experiments.

Vermeulen's melodies of relatively narrow range that turn back in on themselves resemble some of neoclassical Stravinsky's but the chromaticism, rhythmic treatment, length of the melodies, and lack of repetition of melodic cells mark them immediately as different. The smooth and asymmetrically changing melodic contours recall a great deal of prebaroque music, which Vermeulen became interested in from his

first exposure to it in his youth. There are many places in hi
symphonies in which combinations of lines of this kind wit
their independent rhythms even recall specifically the lat
French *ars nova*.

Vermeulen often said that he was carrying on somethin
Debussy and Schoenberg started, e.g. the freeing of musi
from certain restraints such as tonality. As implied earlier, h
was and he wasn't. A more important revolutionary aspect o
his music concerns those places where basically independer
lines, each one going its own way, seem to combine by beir
just "put together" regardless of the exact thematic, harmoni
or contrapuntal results. Within certain wide limits, the orde
ing of the sound events vertically and/or horizontally borde
on being deliberately arbitrary. This procedure brings about
peculiar, almost static effect. The music does not move fo
ward; it is not goal-directed. A large-scale sense of motic
and time is suspended. Parts of sections 2 to 5 in the secor
symphony (including the climax to section 3) are good e
amples of this, and there are more in the other symphonies.

This was all something new in western art in the early 20
century. Matthijs Vermeulen was making an independent ar
most significant contribution to it.

Footnotes to Chapter II

1 Matthijs Vermeulen: "Matthijs Vermeulen: zesde symfonie", in programme notes to the concert by the Utrecht Municipal Orchestra, Utrecht, 25.XI.1959; p. 9.

2 Th. de Crauw: "Matthijs Vermeulen", in *De Muziek*, vol. 4 no. 5, Feb. 1930; p. 208.

3 Matthijs Vermeulen: "Bijdrage tot de muziekgeschiedenis van dezen tijd", in *De Nieuwe Kroniek*, vol. 1 no. 5, 7.V.1921; p. 2. Six plus six plus four make 16, not 14. Could the six second violins have been only four? Someone might have miscopied 6-4-4-2-3 as 6-6-4-2-3.

4 Matthijs Vermeulen: "Werken van Dopper, III—27.X.1916", in *De Eene Grondtoon*, vol. 9 nos. 4-5, 1932, of *De Vrije Bladen*; p. 70.

5 Matthijs Vermeulen: "Bernard Zweers als idee", in *De Eene Grondtoon*; p. 80.

6 Matthijs Vermeulen: "Bijdrage . . . "; p. 3.

7 [Matthijs Vermeulen:] "Vierde symphonie", in programme notes to the concert by the Rotterdam Philharmonic Orchestra, Rotterdam, 30.IX.1949.

8 M[atthijs] V[ermeulen]: "Matthijs Vermeulen: vijfde symphonie", in programme notes to the concert by the Concertgebouw Orchestra, Amsterdam, 12.X.1949; p. 14.

9 See the list of orchestral works at the end of this chapter.

10 Matthijs Vermeulen: "Uitvaart van Mengelberg", in *De Muziek, Dat Wonder* (The Hague: Daamen, 1958); p. 98.

11 Matthijs Vermeulen: "Beschouwingen bij mijn zesde symfonie", in *De Groene Amsterdammer*, vol. 88 no. 49, 5.XII.1959; p. 11.

12 *Ibid.*; p. 9.

13 Matthijs Vermeulen: "Uit de wereld van Mahler", in *De Muziek, Dat Wonder*; p. 76.

14 Matthijs Vermeulen: *Princiepen der Europese Muziek* (Amsterdam: Uitgeversmaatschappij Holland, 1949); p. 148. Of course, the sentiments expressed here and in the two preceding quotations were ideals which Vermeulen did not seek to realize *throughout* any one work: the various levels of chaos and order he kept under large-scale control. A further remark about the "future orchestra" quotation will be found in Chapter VIII.

Vif et net; avec
du mordant

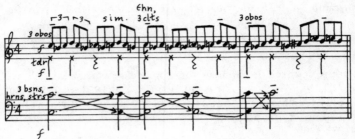

Ex. 1: Symphony No. 4 (p. 1, mm. 1-3)

Ex. 2 (basic rhythms)

♪=160

Ex. 3: Symphony No. 3 (p. 101, m. 5 to p. 102, m. 2)

Très doux et mystérieux;
élargissez

Ex. 4: Symphony No. 4 (p. 175, mm. 1-3)

[Calme mais mobile]

Spn sax,
sop sax

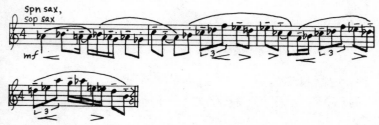

Ex. 5: Symphony No. 5 (p. 144, m. 2 to p. 145, m. 2)

♩=54

Ex. 6: Symphony No. 6 (p. 4, m. 3 to p. 6, m. 4)

Intensif et strident

4 obos, E♭ clts î,
3 clts î, E♭ tpts

Ex. 7: Symphony No. 2 (p. 3, m. 1 to p. 4, m. 1)

Ex. 8: Symphony No. 2 (accompanying chord to ex. 7)

Ex. 9: Symphony No. 2 (changes in upward leaps in the main theme)

Ex. 10: Symphony No. 2 (p. 59, m. 1)

Ex. 11: Symphony No. 2 (final chord)

Ex. 12: Symphony No. 2 (p. 13, m. 4 to p. 15, m. 1)

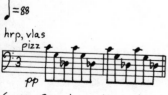

Ex. 13: Symphony No. 2 (p. 25, m. 7 to p. 26, m. 1)

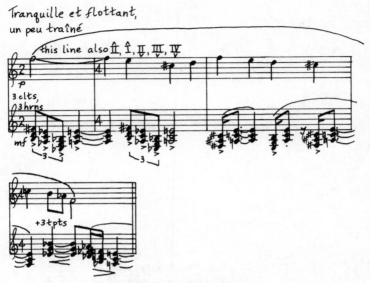

Ex. 14: Symphony No. 2 (p. 34, m. 5 to p. 35, m. 3)

Ex. 15: Symphony No. 2 (p. 81, m. 4 to p. 82, m. 2)

Ex. 16: Symphony No. 2 (p. 98, mm. 1-8)

ORCHESTRAL WORKS BY MATTHIJS VERMEULEN

For an explanation of abbreviations and what is included in this list, see page 19.

SYMPHONY NO.	1, *Symphonia Carminum** (1912-14)
1st prf:	12.III.1919. Richard Heuckeroth, Arnhem Orchestral Society.
2nd prf:	5.V.1964. Bernard Haitink, [Amsterdam] Concertgebouw Orc.
Pbd:	Amsterdam. Stichting Donemus, 1953.
SYMPHONY NO.	2, *Prélude à la Nouvelle Journée** (1919-20)
1st prf:	9.XII.1953. Franz André, Belgian Radio S.O.
Pbd:	Amsterdam. Stichting Donemus, 1951.
SYMPHONY NO.	3, *Thrène et Péan* (1921-22)
1st prf:	24.V.1939. Eduard van Beinum, [Amsterdam] Concertgebouw Orc.
Pbd:	Amsterdam. Stichting Donemus, 1956.
SYMPHONY NO.	4, *Les Victoires* (1940-41)
1st prf:	30.IX.1949. Eduard Flipse, Rotterdam P.O.
Pbd:	Amsterdam. Stichting Donemus, 1947.
SYMPHONY NO.	5, *Les Lendemains Chantants* (1941-44, 45)
1st prf:	12.X.1949. Eduard van Beinum, [Amsterdam] Concertgebouw Orc.
Pbd:	Amsterdam. Stichting Donemus, 1948.
SYMPHONY NO.	6, *Les Minutes Heureuses* (1956-58)
1st prf:	25.XI.1959. Paul Hupperts, Utrecht Municipal Orc.
Pbd:	Amsterdam. Stichting Donemus, 1959.
SYMPHONY NO.	7, *Dithyrambes pour les Temps à Venir** (1963-65)
1st prf:	2.IV.1967. Bernard Haitink, [Amsterdam] Concertgebouw Orc.
Pbd:	Amsterdam. Stichting Donemus, 1965.

OTHER WORKS

two sonatas for cello and piano (1918, 1938), one for violin and piano (1925); string trio (1923); string quartet (1961); several songs (1917, 1941, 1944, 1962); music for Martinus Nijhoff's *De Vliegende Hollander* (1930).

DISCOGRAPHY OF ORCHESTRAL WORKS IN THE MAIN LIST

SYMPHONY NO. 1, *Symphonia Carminum.* Edo de Waart, Rotterdam P.O. Donemus DAVS 7273/1 (with two works by Alphons Diepenbrock).

SYMPHONY NO. 2, *Prélude à la Nouvelle Journée*. Hiroyuki Iwaki, [The Hague] Residentie Orc. a) Donemus DAVS 7374/1 (with Bon: Symphony No. 2). b) Donemus Composers' Voice Special (1976) (in a two-record set with Vermeulen: *Les Filles du Roi d'Espagne* (Louise Verheul, soprano; Jan van der Meer, piano) and works by Diepenbrock, Dresden, Pijper, and Ruyneman).

SYMPHONY NO. 7, *Dithyrambes pour les Temps à Venir*. Bernard Haitink, [Amsterdam] Concertgebouw Orc. Donemus DAVS 6801 (mono) (with works by Diepenbrock and Pijper).

ORCHESTRAL AUTOGRAPH MANUSCRIPTS

These are with the composer's widow. Enquiries should be addressed to Vermeulen's publisher Stichting Donemus.

SELECTED WRITINGS BY MATTHIJS VERMEULEN

De Twee Muzieken Volumes 1 and 2 (Leiden: A.W. Sijthoff, 1918).

"Bijdrage tot de muziekgeschiedenis van dezen tijd", in *De Nieuwe Kroniek*, vol. 1 no. 5, 7.V.1921; pp. 1-4.

Klankbord (vol. 6 nos. 8-9, Aug.-Sep. 1929, of *De Vrije Bladen*).

De Eene Grondtoon (vol. 9 nos. 4-5, 1932, of *De Vrije Bladen*).

Het Avontuur van den Geest (Amsterdam: Amsterdamsche Boek- en Courantmaatschappij, 1947). Translated by Matthijs Vermeulen as *L'Aventure de l'Esprit* (Paris: Editions Renée Lacoste, 1955).

Princiepen der Europese Muziek (Amsterdam: Uitgeversmaatschappij Holland, 1949).

"De atoomwapens en ons geweten", transcript of a speech given 13.II.1955 (Amsterdam: Nederlandse Vredesraad, 1955).

De Muziek, Dat Wonder (The Hague: Daamen, 1958).

"Beschouwingen bij mijn zesde symfonie", in *De Groene Amsterdammer*, vol. 88 no. 49, 5.XII.1959; pp. 9 and 11. Translated by Elisabeth Meijer as "Notes on my sixth symphony", in *Delta*, vol. 4 no. 3, Autumn 1961; pp. 26-35.

"Matthijs Vermeulen: seventh symphony", translated by Ian F. Finlay in *Sonorum Speculum*, no. 29, Winter 1966; pp. 24-36.

"De programma's van het Concertgebouworkest", in *De Groene Amsterdammer*, 21.I.1967; p. 5.

SELECTED WRITINGS BY OTHERS ABOUT VERMEULEN

Th. de Crauw: "Matthijs Vermeulen", in *De Muziek*, vol. 4 no. 5, Feb. 1930; pp. 208-14.

Wouter Paap: "De componist Matthijs Vermeulen", in *Mens en Melodie*, vol. 4 no. 11, Nov. 1949; pp. 329-31.

Wouter Paap: "Nederlandse componisten van deze tijd—XXII. Matthijs Vermeulen", in *Mens en Melodie*, vol. 11 no. 6, June 1956; pp. 162-67.

Ernst Vermeulen: "Composers' gallery—Matthijs Vermeulen", translated by Ian F. Finlay in *Sonorum Speculum*, no. 28, Autumn 1966; pp. 1-9.

Wouter Paap: "In memoriam Matthijs Vermeulen", in *Mens en Melodie*, vol. 12 no. 9, Sep. 1967; pp. 257-62.

Thea Vermeulen-Diepenbrock: "Ter voorkoming van legendevorming", in *Mens en Melodie*, vol. 23 no. 1, Jan. 1968; pp. 11-14.

J. Bernlef: "De zaak-Dreyfus van ons muziekleven", in *Haagse Post*, vol. 58 no. 34, 18.VIII/24.VIII.1971; pp. 48-51. Revised version translated as " 'I've never felt the need of a system' ", in *Key Notes*, no. 3, 1976 no. 1; pp. 35-40.

Reinbert de Leeuw: "Matthijs Vermeulen", in his *Muzikale Anarchie* (Amsterdam: De Bezige Bij, 1973); pp. 52-63. Translated by Sylvia G. Broere-Moore into English with the same title, in *Sonorum Speculum*, no. 52, 1973; pp. 1-10.

Otto Ketting: "Prelude as postlude", in *Key Notes*, no. 3, 1976 no. 1; pp. 42-45.

Vagn Holmboe in 1949

III   Vagn Holmboe and his Symphony No.7

[Music] can expand man's mind, broaden his understanding, and enrich his emotional life, but only when the music itself is a cosmos of co-ordinated powers, when it speaks to both feeling and thought, when chaos does exist, but [is] always overcome.[1]

Vagn Holmboe was born on 20 December 1909 in Horsens, Denmark. He began serious music study at the conservatory in Copenhagen in 1926, where his two chief teachers were Knud Jeppesen (in music theory) and Finn Høffding (in composition). His performing instrument was the viola, although he never played it professionally. In 1930 he studied briefly with Ernst Toch in Berlin. There he also met a Romanian pianist, Meta Graf, whom he married in 1933. In 1933-34 he travelled in Romania, collecting and studying Balkan folk music, which in several ways has remained an important influence on his music to the present.

His first publicly performed composition (a string trio) was heard in 1932, and his first important published composition (a sonata for violin and piano) was printed in 1935. After his Romanian trip, he had returned to Denmark to teach music privately. In the 1930's he also wrote several interesting articles for *Dansk Musiktidsskrift* on such subjects as aesthetics, modern music, Romanian folk music, Arabic music culture, and street songs in Copenhagen.

Holmboe was and still is interested in many "vernacular" ("non-art") musics of the world, even if his active research into them stopped at the end of the 1930's. Through his study of such musics and probably also of pre-17th-century western "cultivated" ("art") music, he came to the conclusion that the major-minor harmonic system, while basically a very sophisticated and useful one, had constricted develop-

[1]   See footnotes p. 63

ment of other musical elements such as melody, rhythm, and phrase construction. In his own compositions he began to modify the major-minor harmonic system and expanded it in chromatic and polymodal directions so as to allow for greater freedom of treatment of these other elements. Some of his works from around this time, such as the Symphony No. 3 (*Sinfonia Rustica*, 1941), are based on actual folk tunes, but gradually he involved himself less with direct quotation of folk material and more with its abstracted essence, in relation to what he perceived as his own western and northern-European cultivated-music traditions.

Probably the most important prize Vagn Holmboe has won among the nearly two dozen awarded him in the past 40-plus years is the first prize in the Danish Royal Orchestra's Scandinavian competition for an orchestral work that was held in 1939. The winning work was his Symphony No. 2. Holmboe tells an amusing story concerning this competition. Apparently, during the early rounds of the judging, the conductor Egisto Tango, who was one of the judges, was away from Denmark. The committee of judges advanced several work to a final round; Holmboe's was not among them. But when Tango returned to Denmark, he demanded to look over all the entries and then went on to insist that while Holmboe's symphony was far from perfect, it was certainly the best composition submitted. The symphony was then reconsidered and given first prize.

The prize was important for both professional and personal reasons. First, it spectacularly brought Holmboe's name to the attention of many people in Denmark who had never heard of him. Newspaper articles about him became frequent; more students wanted to study with him; performers requested works from him; the major Danish orchestras took up his orchestral compositions. Second, the prize money enabled him and his wife to buy land on which to build, so that they might eventually move to a congenial setting, away from the too busy, too noisy capital city, where Holmboe often found it impossible to write music. Shortly after the German invasion, they bought land near Ramløse, about 30 miles from central Copenhagen: a peaceful, sparsely populated spot in gently rolling farm country, not far from a large forest

Lake Arre, and the northwestern coast of Sjælland, the large island that makes up east-central Denmark. Over the course of about 15 years, the Holmboes cleared and shaped the land, planted thousands of trees and other plants, and built two dwellings. They took up residence there in 1953 and have lived there since then.

From 1940 to 1949 Holmboe taught music at the Institute for the Blind in Copenhagen. The decreased opportunities for performances of his works during the war did not prevent him from writing many large works then, including symphonies 3, 4, and 5. None of these symphonies was played before Denmark was liberated. But when they were finally heard, the latter two at least found great success. The fourth, which is for chorus and orchestra and uses a simple, prayerful text written by Holmboe, won a Danish Radio prize and was played at the inaugural concert for a new Danish Radio building. The fifth became widely known via an I.S.C.M. performance in Copenhagen in 1947, and later that same year it generated considerable enthusiasm at a Swedish performance. At that time, a long article about Holmboe and his fifth symphony appeared in Sweden. It was the first one about him of any depth to be published outside Denmark.

During the 1940's he wrote, among much else, four symphonies (no. 6 is from 1947), ten concertos mostly for one to three solo instruments and smaller orchestras, seven cantatas, and string quartets nos. 1 to 3. The cantatas were commissions for celebrations held by various Danish organizations (e.g. City of Horsens, Danish Nursing Council). The quartets were not the first three he had written. Before them there were ten unnumbered others, consisting of "juvenilia" and incomplete quartets which were never published, although some had been performed. All 15 numbered quartets have now been performed; fourteen have been published and eleven recorded. Probably all 15 will be available before long in both mediums. They have been highly regarded in Scandinavia but only rarely performed elsewhere or by non-Scandinavian quartet groups.

In 1947 Holmboe became a music reviewer for *Politiken*, one of the two main Copenhagen daily newspapers. In 1950 he became a teacher at the Royal Conservatory in Copenhagen.

171035

His work for *Politiken* ended in 1955 as he was named professor in theory and composition at the conservatory, a position he held until 1965. He was also active in the Danish Composers' Association from 1942 to 1973. As can be seen, all his major professional activities have taken place in Denmark. The many prizes he has won have almost all been Danish, and his commissions have almost all been Scandinavian.

In 1965 he "retired" into a busy life of full-time composing, aided by a pension and by a large annual grant renewable for life from the government's Cultural Foundation. This grant constituted a very high honour given in recognition of his services to Danish music.

To date, Holmboe has completed about 45 concertos and "symphonic" works.[2] The differences between *concerto* and *symphony* in his usage go well beyond matters of specific form patterns or of presence or absence of specified soloists (two concertos have none). He once wrote about the distinctions as general principles, characteristically naming no composers but really referring to his own work:

> All music in which the component instruments so to speak give up their individuality and adapt themselves in a larger totality where they *sound together* is *symphonic* music; just the opposite is music in which the instruments enter into outright *competition* with each other, where certain instruments step forward; such music is *concerto* music.
>
> In its essence, the symphony is therefore music that is built on synthesis, on continuity, or to say it more fashionably, it is the line and the tension that are crucial for whether a work is symphonic or not; spontaneous contrasts must be subsidiary, if the symphonic line is not going to be covered up or broken. The concerto's essence is, however, play; play between instruments or between dynamic and timbral contrasts; any line, in the symphonic sense, is contrary to the concerto's nature.[3]

Since this characterization is so general, it can not be applied precisely to specific parts of Holmboe's orchestral works chosen randomly. The statement was published in 1944 and does not really apply to some works written recently. But in general it does describe differences in attitude which are reflected in many ways in the concertos and symphonies as whole groups of works, especially those written in the

1940's and 50's. Excellent comparisons in this regard could be made between the Concerto No. 2 (for flute, violin, and small orchestra, 1940) and the fifth symphony (1944), or between the Concerto No. 10 (with no specified soloists, 1945-46) and the sixth symphony (1947). In most cases, the symphonic works are more intense, developmental, and dramatic. They are of larger dimensions and scope, with longer lines and more complex structures.

The ideas in the quotation above concerning synthesis, continuity, and subsidiary nature of contrasts contain the seed of a compositional principle which Holmboe later termed *metamorphosis*, and which is also characteristic more of the symphonies than of the concertos. He once wrote what he considered metamorphosis to be. But again, this was a general statement with many possible specific applications:

> Metamorphosis is based on a process of development that transforms one matter into another, without it losing its identity, its basic characteristics. Metamorphic music is thus by its nature marked by unity, which among other things means that contrasts, however strong they may be, are always made of the same material substance, and that contrasts can indeed be complementary but not dualistic. [4]

In its simplest sense, metamorphosis is thematic metamorphosis: the turning of one theme into another. But Holmboe's music demonstrates that proper consideration of what metamorphosis means even in only his music is an enormous undertaking. Metamorphosis literally signifies "change of shape", but what "change" and "shape" are changes with the shapes of each work. In other writings, Holmboe goes on to say that the starting point (or starting "shape") for some kind of metamorphosis may not be a theme at all: perhaps a motive or group of motives; an interval; a cadence; a timbre; a gesture independent of fixed rhythms, intervals, or timbres; or a series of pitches or pitch classes which may never appear in its basic form at all — as in twelve-tone series. Or perhaps combinations of these items, with emphasis more on one here and another there, so that the question of what the basic starting point of the metamorphosis is may not have a single, simple answer.

Nor do metamorphoses often proceed in predictable ways, or ways easily represented by some kind of diagram. A metamorphosis of a musical idea may even be felt to have taken place when the external shape of that idea has not changed, because a metamorphosis may bring about a new relationship of an old idea to a new context. Regardless of what kinds of metamorphosis go on, metamorphosis in general is a phenomenon of process, a method of creating change, and of realizing multiplicity from a complex unity. One can not really identify details of metamorphosis by investigating stages of development unless one also investigates the many relationships implied by those stages. Thus it is difficult or perhaps impossible to illustrate the details of metamorphosis by discussion of mere isolated music examples. Context is everything: what goes on between and around examples is often as important as any examples themselves.

Metamorphosis can also not be considered a form pattern in the ways that sonata, rondo, fugue, and even variation might be in (primarily) 18th-century music. In Holmboe's music, there is nothing about metamorphosis which predicts or precludes any kind of form pattern or proportions, or degree of repetition, development, sectionalization, contrast, and so on. In this regard it might be compared to serialism as a method of composition, not in serialism's presuppositions about content and ordering of elements in a system, but in its ability to generate music of very different properties. Serialism also implies constant change allied with constant lack of change: a unity of apparent divergences, a continuous development, in fact nearly everything in Holmboe's paragraph about metamorphosis quoted earlier. Nevertheless, Holmboe generally rejected most of the important aspects of serialism as means of composition for himself because he found its methods as he understood them too straitening for the sounds, relationships, and meanings he was interested in.

A most interesting group of works for the study of metamorphosis in Holmboe's music is the four orchestral works to which he gave the subtitle *symphonic metamorphosis*: *Epitaph* (1956), *Monolith* (1960), *Epilog* (1961-62), and *Tempo Variabile* (1971-72). In general characteristics of style, the first three works are closely related, as might be expected because of their close dates of composition. But far more interesting are the many different things which all four have to reveal about metamorphosis, in technical and other senses.

Epitaph is concerned with the dissolution or outright destruction of the main melodic shapes evolved at the work's beginning (mm. 1-10). The third movement is the shortest of the three but seems much longer than its actual clock time because of its extreme density of metamorphic relationships: nearly every gesture in it reflects and recasts so much from the whole work. The main melodic idea from the beginning of *Epitaph* (ex. 1) grows into longer themes throughout it; these can be heard fairly readily to complement each other through their common motivic bases. One of these longer themes begins as ex. 2.

Like *Epitaph*, *Monolith* is built on short motives and is sharply and dramatically defined in its surface rhythmic activity. But its unity is of another kind. Its basis is a twelve-tone series (ex. 3, which may arbitrarily be designated the prime form at transposition level 0). *Monolith* is in fact Holmboe's most serial orchestral work, although it is far from serial throughout. Also, it makes extended use of only a few of the 48 possible series forms, and in fairly simple ways. The series acts as a "fund" from which three main ideas seem to draw their main shapes. One of the most interesting developments to follow in *Monolith* is the evolving prominence of one of these ideas — initially only an unassuming cadential figure (first heard as ex. 4). Its "journeys" and the change in hierarchy among the three main ideas help bring about a kind of metamorphosis of the shape from ex. 4, even though its *physical* shape at the end of the work is very close to what it was at the start.

Epilog is the longest of these four works (about 24½ minutes). Unlike *Epitaph*, its *first* movement is the densest in metamorphic relationships. Another difference between these two compositions is this: the various themes in the first movement of *Epilog* are much more tightly related than those in the third movement of *Epitaph*. One often reads of a movement being totally constructed out of a single motive; the first movement of *Epilog* is one of the few for which such a proposition seems true. (The motive is found in two forms in ex.

5.) This has far-reaching consequences: the succeeding movements must go to great extremes both to get rid of the "influence" of the main motive and, ultimately, to reaccept it, to
integrate it into a world of very different things (see ex. 6,
from near the end of *Epilog*).

Tempo Variabile contrasts greatly in style to the other
three works. Its involvement with metamorphosis is also quite
different, so that the identical subtitle seems a bit misleading,
until one understands that even the term *metamorphosis* has
undergone a large metamorphosis in Holmboe's thinking. The
basic musical materials are frequently wisps and fragments of
sound quite variable in shape from one occasion to another.
Many longer melodies are not fixed enough through repetition and development for an overtly dramatic thematic or
motivic metamorphosis. Metamorphosis does go on, but it
involves intervallic cells, timbres, punctuations, and nonthematic melodic procedures in ways more elusive and less
conclusive than in the earlier works.

Which compositions of Holmboe's are or are not metamorphic in some absolute sense is an engaging matter but can not
be discussed in detail here, partly because it presumes a standard of some kind which has not been established and which it
may be impossible to establish satisfactorily. Metamorphosis
is like tonality: it operates on many musical levels. In any
given musical work, it may be present on some level and
absent on another, or operating in one part of a work and not
so much in another. Thus, the important ultimate questions
regarding metamorphosis do not look for a "yes or no" answer, but rather more detailed explanations involving "how",
"how much", and possibly "why". It is with these concerns in
mind that the following merely preliminary discussion is
offered of Holmboe's seventh symphony. This discussion is
not a metamorphic analysis, but a guide to some of the analytical concepts and concerns which metamorphosis relates to
in what is one of Holmboe's most metamorphic works.

The seventh symphony, from 1950, is the first orchestral
work in which Holmboe reports that he consciously worked
with the problems of metamorphosis. Earlier orchestral works
are involved with them but not on as large a scale or in so detailed a manner. The compositional precedents for the sym-

phony are more readily found in the four major nonorchestral works immediately preceding it, dating from 1948-50: three string quartets and a large piano work *Suono da Bardo*, revealingly subtitled *Symphonic Suite*.

The symphony has a design unique in Holmboe's production: three movements plus coda, with *intermedios* linking them all, the whole playing without pause. The resulting basic pattern is: movement 1, *allegro* — intermedio 1, *andantino* — movement 2, *adagio* — intermedio 2, *andantino* — movement 3, *presto* — intermedio 3, *andantino* — coda, *andante*. It would be erroneous to describe the symphony as being in seven movements, as the intermedios are short and not of the same weight as the other portions.

Ex. 7 is the dramatic opening of the symphony. In this form it is not really a theme. It serves more as a motto, to recur at certain climactic points, and as a source for further musical ideas. The first of these new ideas begins as ex. 8. Already a metamorphosis has taken place. It can be grasped most readily by comparing the notes under M in ex. 7 with ex. 8. Rhythmic alterations, octave transpositions, and changes in dynamics, articulation, and timbre all produce a theme whose emotional character differs strikingly from what was heard in ex. 7. Because of the particular metric placement of the notes in ex. 8, the essential melodic motion comes out as D-E♭-D, which is also important in ex. 7 in the same configuration, but more as the inversion E♭-D-E♭. Thus metamorphosis is already acting on more than one level, i.e. not merely on the level of note-to-adjacent-note. These two examples also suggest a multiple derivation of the metamorphosis. The new idea (ex. 8) may be heard to come from two different earlier ones: from the material under M and from the E♭-D-E♭ idea.

The next two main themes from the first movement are given in exs. 9 and 10. Of great significance in ex. 9 is the opening and closing D-B♭-D. This comes most clearly from the end of ex. 7. Again a dramatic idea has found later expression as part of a more lyrical one. The rest of ex. 9 shows Holmboe's tendency to expand melodic space slowly and fill it in chromatically within a basically diatonic modal framework.

Chiefly because of its accompaniment, change of tonal level

to A, and use of the perfect fourth, the new theme in the violins in ex. 10 sounds more contrasting than it really is. The shapes X, Y, and Z from ex. 9 are found transposed down a fourth (not always a perfect fourth). Moreover, the repeated interval of the perfect fourth encloses the rest of the ex. 10 melody (which, apart from its beginning and end, does not emphasize perfect fourths) just as the D-B^b-D major third encloses the rest of ex. 9 (which, apart from its beginning and end, does not emphasize major thirds). Thus the two melodies are also linked structurally. Within Q' (ex. 10), the A-F-A major third also recalls immediately the opening and closing of ex. 9. And an additional relationship to ex. 7 is found in Q'. The major third plus minor second within a *perfect fourth*, noted as Q in ex. 7, becomes a major third plus minor second within a *major third* in Q' (ex. 10): the minor second is "inside" rather than "outside" the major third.

The opposition between melodic fourths and the other main interval classes (which are seconds and thirds), upon which the whole structure of the sixth symphony is founded, is of little importance in the first movement of the seventh symphony beyond what has just been illustrated. The theme from ex. 10 does not even return. Most of the melodic development in the first movement involves ex. 9. The vertical sonorities of the movement and indeed of the whole symphony are basically tertian, and there are several passages which also emphasize seconds, especially minor seconds. Vertically, the fourth is the least important of the interval classes, except inasmuch as the interval of the fifth is the sum of two thirds.

The two chief melodic lines of the first four measures of the first movement's climax are shown as ex. 11. This example reveals another possibility of metamorphosis: the contrapuntal combination of two previous ideas (here exs. 7 and 9) to create something quite new. This is not merely development by simultaneous presentation of previously separate material. The dramatic, unsettled ex. 7 and the more lyrical and relaxed ex. 9, by joining here in a grotesque dance, reveal a new common ground for both. Ex. 11 makes explicit implicit potentials in exs. 7 and 9, very much increasing their emotional and structural impact.

The basic material of all three intermedios is ex. 12, drawn from the first intermedio. A description of the D-C-D motive as just another variant of the beginning of exs. 9 or 10 would miss a great deal. In connection with those examples, W'' (ex. 12) continues a pattern begun by W (ex. 9) and W' (ex. 10). The descent and return of a third (in W) and of a fourth (in W') is developed further in the top line of W'' by the descent and return there of a second. This main motive has now been heard with each of the three largest interval classes.[5]

The possible sources of ex. 12 are not exhausted by consideration of W and W' from exs. 9 and 10. The accompaniment to ex. 10 is another source, although its relation to ex. 12 may be considered not fully revealed until much later — near the end of the second movement (p. 55), when a similar brass line makes the relationship clearer. Metamorphosis in Holmboe's music often does this: hints of relationships, possibilities, ambiguities may be refined and redefined by earlier or later events far removed from each other in time and character.

The first intermedio is a quiet, dream-like transition between the first and second movements. The second movement begins *adagio* but increases its speed in several stages to a *moderato* which is still felt as a relatively slow tempo because of long metric units and a slow "rhythm of events". The end of the movement is again *adagio*. It makes use of fugato, which is extremely rare in Holmboe's music. Here it is put to a rather unusual use: the thematic saturation acts to dissolve the movement, rather than build up tension.

The theme of this fugato is the same as the theme found at the opening of the movement, which is given in ex. 13. It is another version of ex. 9, but like ex. 10 centres around A rather than D. Like ex. 10, the perfect fourth is prominent, but only descending. One can scarcely point to a reason for this, but a *foreshadowing* of these descending perfect fourths, and their position of following ascending and/or descending thirds, may be heard in the bass accompaniment line preceding ex. 11 (see ex. 14 for this bass line).

The role of this accompaniment shows that metamorphosis in the symphony is not restricted to relationships among only the major foreground melodies. One of the principal accompaniment figures in the second movement begins as ex. 15. The melodic ascent in four notes of equal rhythmic value often changes its harmonic function and with it the arrangement of major seconds and minor seconds. But the ascent by conjoined seconds (whether major or minor) remains characteristic. Since its basic outline is so straightforward, the addition of just one more note (whether in the same direction or not) changes its structure significantly. One of these simple additions in fact leads to a second main theme in this movement (ex. 16). Less simple but still related to ex. 15 are the rearrangements of the four notes which produce exs. 17 and 18. Ex. 17 is a basic accompaniment in the third movement; ex. 18 is the motive heard in rapid imitation at the symphony's climax, also in the third movement. They are but two of the several important near-relations to ex. 15. As the symphony progresses, relationships among these initially simple musical ideas multiply very quickly. Each new development affects the understanding of nearly all the others.

The second intermedio functions much like the first. But there is less stability at the end of the second one, because of the simultaneous activity there of horn and tuba lines that have little to do with each other. The former represents the world of the minor second and the latter the world of the perfect fourth.

The third movement keeps up a rapid pulse through several climaxes, culminating in the one referred to earlier. Previous ideas are constantly heard in both new and older forms, giving forth new character and meaning. Some previous musical ideas are now familiar enough that Holmboe may use only a brief allusion to them in order to recall them in their entirety. Indeed, many aural images seem to flash by as if in a dream, scarcely prepared or followed up, recalled in a succession of incomplete but powerful thoughts which only *seem* to be unrelated. The complex network of metamorphoses already established makes all this possible.

One particularly good example of this phenomenon can be found on p. 86, where there is very little activity. Previous lines are "flattened out" into dissolved shapes which would hardly be recognizable as representing more distinguished shapes if the progression to this point had not been carefully arranged. Suddenly high F#s ring out in the woodwinds and celesta (see ex. 19). The harmonic setting there has little to do with m. 7 of ex. 7, but a reference to that point is perceived because of the nearly identical woodwind scoring and because of the cymbal stroke accompanying the F#s, which also accompanied the first beat in m. 7 of ex. 7. The metamorphic flattening out of other significant melodic lines is partly what makes this event work.

Ex. 20 is a theme new in the third movement. Disregarding transposition, it is repeated in the same form many times in this movement, as if to challenge the listener to discover its derivation from other themes and motives. It relates to so many of them, both already heard and yet to come (including the F#s in ex. 19) that its structural meaning reaches far beyond its own immediate domains.[6] Most striking, perhaps, is the interval class of the prime in W''': this completes the pattern set up earlier by the several W-motives in exs. 9, 10, and 12. With ex. 20, this motive has then been heard with all the possible basic interval classes (prime, second, third, fourth).

In the third movement, new relationships continue to be built involving the opposition of the interval class of the fourth to the class of seconds and thirds, an opposition which might be termed a musical idea in itself. There is no *confrontation* between the fourths and the others, but they continue to interact in new ways. The fourth becomes part of a new version of the intermedio music, which is heard prominently several times within the third movement. New variations of the two most important themes of the symphony, ex. 9 (from the first movement and without the fourths) and ex. 13 (from the second movement and with the fourths), are heard in this order: ex. 9 followed by ex. 13, and then ex. 13 followed by ex. 9. The two pairs are symmetrically placed about the movement's climax. And finally, the pattern marked R in ex. 13, the non-fourth motive found in a spot in that example where the descending fourths might be expected to recur, is heard three times at a very significant structural point together with ascending and descending perfect fourths in the bass (see ex. 21). The opposing fourths and non-fourths from the one theme (ex. 13) gain new life as separate but interdependent members of one texture.

The third movement comes to a final rest on a long D major chord,. *diminuendo*. The coda ends similarly, raising the question of why the symphony does not end with the third movement. The answers lie in a consideration of what the coda does. First, it brings the music back to the domain of the non-fourth interval classes, which the end of the third movement seems deliberately too short to do. Second, the coda's link with the preceding intermedio (no. 3) is the strongest one yet: the growing importance of the intermedios as a group is confirmed. Third, the symphony's opening motto (in ex. 7) comes back with much the same character at the end of the first and second movements, but not the third. The coda completes this structural gap in a most forceful way.

Finally, the coda fulfills a harmonic tendency which has been denied throughout virtually the entire symphony. Right from the opening motto, the pitch class B^b lives an almost independent existence in the key of D. In fact, partly because of the B^{b}s, the tonality of the first six measures of ex. 7 is not definite at all. Over and over again in structurally significant lines, B^b does not resolve down to the fifth step in the key of D. This remarkable "refusal" is especially noticeable in the biggest climaxes of the first and third movements. The resolution to A in the key of D begins to happen in the third movement, but its complete significance is not brought out until the fourth-last measure of the symphony (m. 3 of ex. 22). The march-like alternation of D and B^b, begun at the end of ex. 7, returns. The last B^{b}s move to As over the closing pedal D. The effect of this simple progression in this scoring at this point in the symphony seems beyond the ability of mere words to characterize adequately. It provides a powerful closing to a powerful composition.

Footnotes to Chapter III

1 Vagn Holmboe: *Mellemspil* (Copenhagen: Wilhelm Hansen, 1961); p. 51.

2 "Symphonic" is intended here primarily as *compositionally symphonic* in the senses suggested in chapters I and VIII. The "about 45" disregards concertos and symphonic works among the more than 75 early works predating op. 1 of 1935.

3 Vagn Holmboe: "Symfoni, koncert og nutidens musik", in *Levende Musik*, vol. 3 no. 9, 1944; pp. 233-34.

4 Vagn Holmboe: *Mellemspil*; pp. 43-44.

5 The interval class of the prime will be discussed in connection with ex. 20.

6 It is worth noting that exs. 8, 18, and 20 are three very different creations built entirely of (unordered) conjoined minor seconds.

Allegro con fuoco

Ex. 1: Epitaph (p. 2, mm. 2-4)

Andante tranquillo

Ex. 2: Epitaph (p. 40, mm. 1-3)

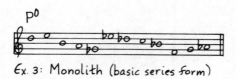

Ex. 3: Monolith (basic series form)

Allegro con forza

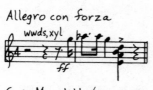

Ex. 4: Monolith (p. 4, mm. 2-3)

Allegro

Ex. 5: Epilog (p. 3, mm. 1-3)

Ex. 6: Epilog (p.143, m.3 to p. 145, m.4)

Allegro con fuoco

Ex. 7: Symphony No. 7 (p. 1, m.1 to p.2, m.2)

Allegro con fuoco

Ex. 8: Symphony No. 7 (p.2, m.6 to p.3, m.1)

Allegro con fuoco

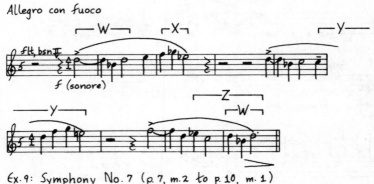

Ex. 9: Symphony No. 7 (p. 7, m.2 to p. 10, m. 1)

[Allegro]

Ex. 10: Symphony No. 7 (p. 20, m.1 to p. 21, m.3)

[Allegro]

Ex. 11: Symphony No. 7 (p. 32, mm. 2-5)

Andantino

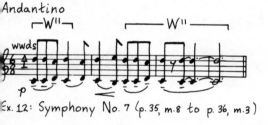

Ex. 12: Symphony No. 7 (p. 35, m. 8 to p. 36, m. 3)

Adagio

Ex. 13: Symphony No. 7 (p. 39, m. 2 to p. 40, m. 2)

[Allegro]

Ex. 14: Symphony No. 7 (p. 30, m.5 to p. 31, m. 4)

Ex. 15: Symphony No. 7 (p. 40, m. 2)

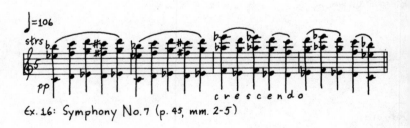

Ex. 16: Symphony No. 7 (p. 45, mm. 2-5)

Presto

Ex. 17: Symphony No. 7 (p. 65, m. 6)

Allegro moderato

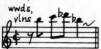

Ex. 18: Symphony No. 7 (p. 109, m. 3)

[Vivace]

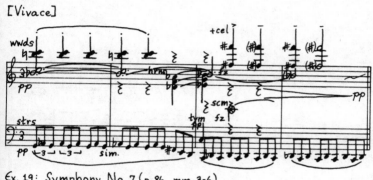

Ex. 19: Symphony No. 7 (p. 86, mm. 3-6)

[Vivace]

Ex. 20: Symphony No. 7 (p. 75, mm. 2-4)

Ex. 21: Symphony No. 7 (p. 113, mm. 1-7)

Ex. 22: Symphony No. 7 (p. 129, mm. 1-6)

ORCHESTRAL WORKS BY VAGN HOLMBOE (from 1935 onwards)

For an explanation of abbreviations and what is included in this list, see
page 19.

SUITE FOR CHAMBER ORCHESTRA NO. 1, op. 1 (1935)
1st prf: 30.III.1936. Ebbe Hamerik, D.U.T. Orc.

SYMPHONY NO. 1, op. 4 (1935)
1st prf: 21.II.1938. Thomas Jensen, Århus City Orc.

SUITE FOR CHAMBER ORCHESTRA NO. 2, op. 6 (1935-36)
1st prf: 20.IV.1939. Erik Tuxen, cdr.

SUITE FOR CHAMBER ORCHESTRA NO. 3, op. 11 (1936)
1st prf: 23.XI.1938. Georg Høeberg, D.U.T. Orc.

SYMPHONY NO. 2, op. 15 (1938-39)
1st prf: 5.XII.1939. Egisto Tango, [Danish] Royal Orc.

SYMPHONY NO. 3, *Sinfonia Rustica*, op. 25 (1941)
1st prf: 12.VI.1948. Svend Christian Felumb, Tivoli Concert
                Hall Orc.

SYMPHONIC OVERTURE, op. 28 (1941)
1st prf: 13.IV.1943. Emil Reesen, Copenhagen Concert Soci-
                ety Orc.

SYMPHONY NO. 4, *Sinfonia Sacra*, op. 29 (1941, rev. 45)
1st prf: 11.IX.1945. Erik Tuxen, cdr.; Danish Radio S.O.;
                Danish Radio Chorus; Thorkild Roose, reader.

SYMPHONY NO. 5, op. 35 (1944)
1st prf: 16.VI.1945. Lavard Friisholm, Tivoli Concert Hall
                Orc.
Pbd: Copenhagen. Viking, 1947.

CONCERTO NO. 8, *Sinfonia Concertante*, op. 38 (1945)
1st prf: 26.X.1954. Thomas Jensen, Danish Radio S.O.
Pbd: Copenhagen. Viking, no date.

CONCERTO NO. 10, op. 40 (1945-46)
1st prf: 26.IV.1946. Lavard Friisholm, Randers City Orc.
Pbd: Copenhagen. Viking, 1959.

SYMPHONY NO. 6, op. 43 (1947)
1st prf: 8.I.1948. Erik Tuxen, Danish Radio S.O.
Pbd: Copenhagen. Viking, 1949.

SYMPHONY NO. 7, op. 50* (1950)
1st prf: 18.X.1951. Nikolay Malko, Danish Radio S.O.
Pbd: Copenhagen. Viking, 1951.

CHAMBER SYMPHONY NO. 1, op. 53 (1951)
1st prf: 9.III.1951. Lavard Friisholm, Collegium Musicum.
Pbd: Copenhagen. Viking, 1958.

SYMPHONY NO.8, *Sinfonia Boreale*, op. 56* (1951-52)
1st prf: 5.III.1953. Paul Kletzki, Danish Radio S.O.
Pbd: Copenhagen. Viking, 1955.

TRÆET, op. 62 (1953)
1st prf: 5.VI.1975. Lavard Friisholm, cdr.; Randers City Orc.;
              Randers City Chorus.

SINFONIA IN MEMORIAM, op. 65 (1954-55)
1st prf: 5.V.1955. Erik Tuxen, Danish Radio S.O.

EPITAPH (*Symphonic Metamorphosis*), op. 68 (1956)
1st prf: 28.XII.1956. Stanford Robinson, B.B.C. S.O.
Pbd: Copenhagen. Viking, 1958.

KAIROS, op. 73 (1957, 57, 58-59, 62) (See note)
1st prf: 1958, 58, 62, 64. See note.
Pbd: Copenhagen. Wilhelm Hansen, 1958, 58, 60, 64.
              See note.
Note: for strings only. *Kairos* consists of four works titled
              Sinfonia I, II, III, and *IV*, which were written, per-
              formed, and published separately in numerical order
              in the years indicated above. When performed as a
              unit, a special order of the movements is prescribed.
              Kairos has not been performed this way but was pub-
              lished this way by Hansen in 1964.

CANTATA NO. 12 (1958-59)
1st prf: 11.IX.1959. Per Dreier, cdr.; Århus City Orc.; Jutland
              Academic Chorus; Århus Student Singers; Else Mar-
              grete Gardelli, mezzo-soprano; Mogens Wedel, bari-
              tone; Thorkild Bjørnvig, reader.

MONOLITH (*Symphonic Metamorphosis*), op. 76 (1960)
1st prf: 9.IX.1960. Per Dreier, Århus City Orc.
Pbd: Copenhagen. Wilhelm Hansen, 1967.

EPILOG (*Symphonic Metamorphosis*), op. 80 (1961-62)
1st prf: 23.XI.1962. Johan Hye-Knudsen, Gothenburg S.O.
Pbd: Copenhagen. Wilhelm Hansen, 1968.

REQUIEM FOR NIETZSCHE, op. 84 (1963-64)
1st prf: 26.XI.1964. Poul Jørgensen, cdr.; Danish Radio S.O.;
              Danish Radio Chorus; Niels Brincker, tenor; Odd
              Wolstad, baritone.

SYMPHONY NO.9, op. 95 (1967-68, rev. 69)
1st prf: 19.XII.1968. Herbert Blomstedt, Danish Radio S.O.

CHAMBER SYMPHONY NO. 2, op. 100 (1968)
1st prf: 20.I.1969. Lavard Friisholm, Collegium Musicum.

CHAMBER SYMPHONY NO. 3, *Frise*, op. 103a (1969-70)
1st prf: 14.X.1970. Jens Schrøder, Ålborg City Orc.

SYMPHONY NO.10, op. 105* (1970-71, rev. 72)
1st prf: 27.I.1972. Sixten Ehrling, Detroit S.O.
Pbd: Copenhagen. Wilhelm Hansen, 1976.

TEMPO VARIABILE (*Symphonic Metamorphosis*), op. 108 (1971-72)
1st prf: 24.V.1972. Karsten Andersen, [Bergen] Harmonien
                  Orc.

BEATUS PARVO, op. 117 (1973)
1st prf: 19.X.1975. Hugo Andersson, cdr.; Råå Amateur
                  Chorus; Råå Amateur Orc.
Pbd: Copenhagen. Wilhelm Hansen, 1975 (vocal score only).

DIAFORA, op. 118 (1973-74)
1st prf: 27.IV.1975. Ørnulf Boye-Hansen, Oslo Chamber Orc.
Note: for strings only.

OTHER WORKS (from 1935 onwards)

many concertos and concertinos; 15 string quartets (1948 to 78); three
sonatas for violin and piano (1935, 39, 65); many other chamber works;
three piano suites (1949-50, 65, 68); operas *Lave og Jon* (1946-48) and
Kniven (1959-60); ballet *Den Galsindede Tyrk* (1942-44); many cantatas and song cycles, accompanied and unaccompanied; incidental
music; music for children.

DISCOGRAPHY OF ORCHESTRAL WORKS IN THE MAIN LIST

SYMPHONY NO.7. John Frandsen, Danish Radio S.O. DGG DMA
018 (with works by P. Nørgård and Gudmundsen-Holmgreen).

SYMPHONY NO.8. Jerzy Semkow, [Danish] Royal Orc. a) Fona M7
(mono) and S7. b) Turnabout TV 34168S (with P. Nørgård: *Kon-
stellationer*).

SYMPHONY NO.10. Sixten Ehrling, Gothenburg S.O. Caprice CAP
1116 (with Nystroem: *Sinfonia Breve*).

ORCHESTRAL AUTOGRAPH MANUSCRIPTS

Most of these are with the composer, his publisher Edition Wilhelm
Hansen, or at the Danish Royal Library music division. Enquiries
should be addressed to the latter two.

SELECTED WRITINGS BY VAGN HOLMBOE

"Lidt om moderne musik", in *Dansk Musiktidsskrift*, vol. 11 no. 1, Jan. 1936; pp. 21-24.

"Gadesangen i København", in *Dansk Musiktidsskrift*, vol. 13 no. 8, Oct. 1938; pp. 171-79.

"Symfoni, koncert og nutidens musik", in *Levende Musik*, vol. 3 no. 9, 1944; pp. 233-38.

"Tre symfonier", in Ingmar Bengtsson, ed.: *Modern Nordisk Musik* (Stockholm: Natur och Kultur, 1957).

"On form and metamorphosis", in John Beckwith and Udo Kasemets, eds.: *The Modern Composer and His World* (Toronto: University of Toronto Press, 1961); pp. 134-40.

Mellemspil (Copenhagen: Wilhelm Hansen, 1961).

SELECTED WRITINGS BY OTHERS ABOUT VAGN HOLMBOE

Helmer Nørgård: "Vagn Holmboe, nordboen", in *Nordisk Musikkultur*, vol. 2 no. 2, June 1953; pp. 50-53.

Bo Wallner: *Vår Tids Musik i Norden* (Stockholm: Nordiska Musikförlaget, 1968); pp. 160-69.

Thorkild Bjørnvig: "Ord og musik", in *Dansk Musiktidsskrift*, vol. 45 no. 7, 1969; pp. 146-49.

Poul Nielsen: "Nogle bemærkninger til Vagn Holmboes metamorfosebegreb", in Jens Brincker et al.: *Til Professor, Dr. Phil. Nils Schiørring på Hans Tres Års Fødselsdag den 8. April 1970 — En Samling Kortere Musikhistoriske og Teoretiske Bidrag . . .* (Copenhagen: privately printed, 1970).

Paul Rapoport: *Vagn Holmboe: A Catalogue of His Music, Discography, Bibliography, Essays* (London: Triad Press, 1974).

Paul Rapoport: *Vagn Holmboe's Symphonic Metamorphoses* (unpublished Ph.D. thesis for the University of Illinois at Urbana-Champaign [Illinois, U.S.A.], 1975).

Havergal Brian in the mid-1920's

IV Havergal Brian and his Symphony No. 1, *The Gothic*

Here we are living amongst young composers who rebel about their names not being mentioned, or mentioned in the wrong order, and whose works they say are unduly neglected. Yet many old composers are still waiting their chance to show what they can do, and some of them mean it.[1]

Havergal Brian died on 28 November 1972, two months and one day before his 97th birthday. (He was born in Dresden, Staffordshire on 29 January 1876.) At his death, 17 of his 32 symphonies had never been played, there were no commercial records of his music, and no major work of his had been published in 40 years. Two books that had appeared about him were out of print (Reginald Nettel's *Ordeal by Music* (1945) and a small, limited-edition book published by Triad Press in 1969), and a third one nearly so (another Triad Press book, published in 1972).[2]

Four years later, by the end of 1976, only five of his symphonies remained unheard, including three which, having been taped in 1976, were still to be broadcast. Three legitimate and two pirated records made up entirely of Brian's music had been issued. Many works, including several symphonies, had been published for the first time (by Musica Viva). The legendary Symphony No. 1, *The Gothic*, had been reprinted (by Cranz), even if in an edition of only 100 copies. Four new full-length books had been published about Brian, each one changing considerably the state of Brian research. And a Havergal Brian Society had been started.[3]

The frequency of activities relating to Brian's music increased from the end of 1972 to the end of 1976 as a result of his death and in connection with celebrations of his centenary. Two major events were the direct result of his death.

---

[1] See footnotes p. 96

First, in early 1973 Malcolm MacDonald was able to examine and temporarily catalogue the items Brian left at his last residence, principally manuscript sketches. While he was alive, Brian was generally unwilling to let anyone examine these. Second, beginning with Brian's funeral on 4 December 1972, a number of events took place which made Kenneth Eastaugh's book possible (see below) and led to a radically new understanding of Brian's life and the circumstances of many of his works. Principally, these events consisted of sudden revelations about his first marriage and its breakdown, and of the appearance of many letters he wrote to his friends Granville Bantock and Robert Simpson.[4]

The most obvious events connected with the centenary were the continued presentation of Brian's orchestral music in performance: six of the symphonies alone were heard for the first time in 1976. But these performances did not suddenly occur only because of the centenary. They were a result of over 30 years of work by many people.

Brian enjoyed some success in Britain as a composer in the decade before the first world war. Thereafter, however, his new works were played very rarely. From the spring of 1922 to the end of January 1954, the only first performances of his orchestral works were of three excerpts from an opera (in the 1920's and 30's) and a short "comedy overture" (in 1950). The reasons for this decline are not completely clear, but they probably resulted from Brian's own dislike of the very difficult routine required to get his music performed, the devastating effect of the first world war on British musical life, and possibly the events surrounding the breakup of his first marriage. Moreover, between the two world wars, he was interested in writing for large or very large orchestras, which made performances even more unlikely, especially during the depression. Brian may also have made a few enemies with his bold and honest music criticism, which often attacked those in musical power in Britain for not doing enough to advance the causes of new music.

The revival of interest in him which began in the 1950's was due partly to Nettel's book mentioned earlier, and more directly to the work of Robert Simpson in the B.B.C.'s Music Division. Without his persistence in bringing Brian's music to the attention of others, it is doubtful that so much of it would have been discovered so soon, if at all. It also seems that Simpson's strong interest and the resulting performances of Brian's music gave Brian renewed energy, without which he might not have written as much as he did in the last 21 of his composing years (1947-68): four operas, two concertos, 27 symphonies, and a half-dozen other works.

Towards the end of the 1960's, Graham Hatton, Lewis Foreman, and Malcolm MacDonald became actively involved with Brian's music. They may be considered the most important people behind a second wave of interest in it. Hatton, a librarian, has acquired rights to much of Brian's music and has published many of his works under his Musica Viva imprint. He has also edited an enormous number of scores and parts for performances and recordings, and has done a great deal of research into many aspects of Brian's life and works. Foreman, also a librarian, has copied parts and overseen their production for performances of Brian's music which he has organized with some smaller London orchestras. His Triad Press published the two small books noted earlier, one of which he edited. He has written articles about Brian and prepared a catalogue of works (for Nettel's newer biography of Brian; see below). He also wrote a book about the performances of Brian's orchestral music (see below) and was responsible for the discovery of 15 Brian manuscripts, of which 14 were in Brian's handwriting, at the publisher J. and W. Chester in 1974. MacDonald, a free-lance writer, editor, and arranger, has assisted in many ways with concerts and recordings, has reconstructed and arranged music from Brian's operas, and has written many programme notes, prefaces, articles, reviews, and broadcast talks. His 1972 Triad Press book on Brian is being superseded by a multivolume study of Brian's music, of which the first part appeared in 1974.

The four above-mentioned books which appeared after Brian's death, in 1974 and 1976, are the major secondary sources available for the study of Brian's life and music. The full references follow:

1 Malcolm MacDonald: *The Symphonies of Havergal Brian* Volume 1 (London: Kahn and Averill, 1974).

2 Lewis Foreman: *Havergal Brian and the Performance of His Orchestral Music—A History and Sourcebook* (London: Thames Publishing, 1976).

3 Reginald Nettel: *Havergal Brian and His Music* (London: Dennis Dobson, 1976).

4 Kenneth Eastaugh: *Havergal Brian—The Making of a Composer* (London: George G. Harrap and Co., 1976).

None alone is sufficient. Each has a different approach and object, and different strengths and weaknesses. MacDonald's book, a detailed exploration of the first twelve symphonies, consists chiefly of colourful and personal descriptions of the music movement by movement. Foreman's book is basically a bibliographic documentation of the events surrounding every orchestral performance he could trace of Brian's music. Nettel's and Eastaugh's books are both biographies, and both emphasize the years up to about 1927. Otherwise they differ. Nettel reservedly tries to create a balanced view of Brian, with some consideration of the music included; Eastaugh does not discuss the music and concentrates on negative aspects of Brian's character in order to correct widely held ideas about him.

MacDonald's book is the most out-of-date in biographical and bibliographical details, but his first two chapters still form the best succinct introduction to Brian in general and his work up to the 1920's in particular. His chapters 3 to 14 deal with the symphonies dating from 1919 to 1957. He describes his approach as "primarily (but by no means exclusively) descriptive, for, at present, general knowledge of Brian's music is hardly such as to render description superfluous".[5]

The main reservation about this approach and its realization in the book is that it leaves readers at times bewildered. So much information is presented that it all can not possibly be taken in, even with the help of the numerous music examples. After a while, if one does not know most of the music already, one can no longer read about instruments, climaxes, keys, themes, textures, etc. without tiring of trying in vain to imagine the sound and significance of what is being discussed. It appears, rather, that this book was directed towards readers who might some day be able to combine at will listening to

*Page 71 of Brian's autograph manuscript of the vocal score/
short score of Part II of* The Gothic *(from the fifth of the
symphony's six movements), with additions not in
Brian's hand.*

or reading this music with reading the commentaries. When
the book was published, only a few of the twelve symphonies
were readily obtainable on records or in print. However, because more have been issued since then, MacDonald's book
has increased in usefulness with its age. It will also be valuable
as a basis for a more general consideration of the symphonies
and their significance, promised for a future volume, and
much needed.

Not all the writing is about technical musical details. Mac-
Donald's strong imagination often produces metaphorical
references, although not usually as extended as this:

> Then, without warning, an astonishing, enigmatic pianissimo
> chord stares at us, sphinx-like and inscrutable, from full brass. It
> could be the dominant of C flat, but its identity is obscured by
> added notes and wide spacing and somewhere within it a drum
> softly sounds a repeated B-flat. It hangs there, athwart the music,
> utterly static and mysterious. So might some gigantic supernova
> shine out of the depths of space, a cold, far-off, incomprehensible
> radiance, yet signifying the deaths of stars and worlds.[6]

There are too many metaphors in this passage, with implications that are too programmatic. Yet anyone who knows the
sound referred to (near the end of the tenth symphony) will
respond to this characterization and probably find that it says
something deep and true that could hardly be set forth in
more analytical terms. There is real life in the writing throughout the book, and an enthusiasm for Brian's music which is
sometimes overdone but always sincere. Analytical minds
will be put off by the prose style and the somewhat unfo-
cussed presentations, and non-musicians will be trapped by
them because they will not be able to follow the musical arguments. But there is a vast middle ground of readers who,
while probably not able to get a great deal out of an orchestral score, will be able to use the book to deepen their understanding of the individual symphonies, if and when they are
able to hear them repeatedly.

The 138 music examples are immaculately written (by Mac-
Donald himself) and printed and contain but few errors. The
misspellings of words in them come from Brian's manuscripts
and should have been ascribed to the sources, or better still,

eliminated. Lack of tempo indications and time signatures on most examples, and of page, rehearsal, or measure numbers on all of them, makes them much less useful than they might have been.

Lewis Foreman's book was the first to consistently attack and answer questions concerning who played Brian's orchestral music, where, when, and to some extent why. The great amount of research he did in numerous archives is reflected by the bibliographic detail the book presents. The basis of the book may be considered to be the first two appendices, which list the performances chronologically by dates of performance and dates of composition respectively. (Thus "1907 12 Jan" is the first entry in Appendix 1, for the first performance of any of Brian's orchestral music; and "1901" is the first entry in Appendix 2, as that is the given date of composition of the earliest known work of Brian's ever to have been heard, i.e. Psalm 23, first performed in 1973.)

The main body of the book is a fuller treatment of many of the listed performances. The whole study certainly achieves its stated aim:

> to document the performances, to evoke the atmosphere and circumstances of them—with photographs wherever possible—and to provide a source-book of reviews and other written documents on which later commentators on Brian may draw.[7]

Writers who have exaggerated in the past by suggesting that Brian's music lay unperformed from the first world war to the 1950's can now read of the approximately two dozen occasions on which his orchestral music was heard in Britain between 1918 and 1953. Of course, this still does not amount to very many performances, the more unfortunate because they involved only six independent works plus three excerpts from the opera The Tigers, and because no major work written after the first world war was heard during this time. It is thus the book's three chapters on this period of neglect (from the war to 1949) which are the most revealing, not merely for what was played and not played, but for what Brian without success tried to have played. In particular, the B.B.C. Written Archives Centre at Caversham is full of rejection notices from those years.

These chapters, like the others, reproduce fascinating programme notes, publishers' announcements, photographs, letters, newspaper and journal articles, and excerpts from manuscripts and published music. The reviews quoted seem representative and thus, predictably, mostly vague and vacuous. Foreman's commentary is mainly limited to discussing concisely important aspects of the performances, such as background to compositions or concerts in question, Brian's involvement in them, and reasons for believing certain concerts took place despite lack of written record of them. Chapters 8 and 9, covering 1960 to 1975, are full of valuable information about preparation and execution of complicated concerts and recordings, several of which Foreman was directly involved in.

The major problem with the book is that it gives the appearance of having been put together in a bit of a hurry. There are misprints and inconsistencies which lower the book's value as a dependable source for future study. The footnote numbers in the body of Chapter 5 proceed as nos. 1, 2, 3, 7, 4; in the appendix containing the actual footnotes, the mysterious no. 7 does not appear. A more serious problem occurs on p. 40, where a quoted advertisement and a quoted review both contradict what Foreman gives as the dates and conductors of Brian's *Festal Dance*. The date of the first B.B.C. broadcast (1 October 1974) of Brian's 23rd symphony is not to be found: both appendices 1 and 2 have it wrong, the reference to the date on p. 92 is misleading, and the one on p. 94 is right although not specific enough. Appendix 2 also gives the wrong performance (of the four that were done of this work in 1973) as having been broadcast. The index to the book contains some errors of reference and alphabetization.

Reginald Nettel knew Brian longer than any of the other authors did. He met him originally during the second world war when he was engaged in writing two books, the second of which was *Ordeal by Music*. This book formed the basis of his new biography. The newer book makes free use of the older one: its Part I constitutes a revision of *Ordeal by Music* with much quoted verbatim from it. This Part I covers about five-eighths of Brian's life, but the narrative seems to stop at the end of it or a short way into Part II, because the continuity in Part II is disrupted by mostly independent discussions of the music. These are far too short and superficial to be of much use. The book would likely have been better had Nettel omitted many of them and related more about Brian's life from his point of view, especially from the 1930's onward. Characteristics of certain works might still have been mentioned to illustrate points about Brian and his milieu and the complex interactions between them.

It is thus Part I which is more useful. In it, Brian's role in the life of the Potteries emerges vividly, as do the characters and achievements of many of those he came into contact with. Nettel's background as a social music historian and his experiences of life and music in Brian's home area contribute to a lively and insightful discussion of some sociomusical settings the understanding of which is essential for any understanding of Brian.

But partly because of Nettel's identification and association with Brian, and partly because of the relatively nonscholarly approach he takes, it is frequently impossible to tell whose point of view is being represented — Nettel's, Brian's, or another's — and under what circumstances that point of view was expressed if it is not Nettel's. Trouble ensues in the presentation of dialogue whose source is unidentified, as readers can not tell how real such dialogue is or who helped shape it. There is also a report (pp. 158-59) involving Beethoven manuscripts. The interpretation of this report might affect understanding of Brian's methods of composition. But there is no way of knowing whether the ideas expressed are Nettel's, Brian's, or some combination.

Another disadvantage for anyone wishing to go further into many of the events described is that they have no dates ascribed to them, not even a year. Other problems in the book's organization also make events difficult to sort out.

The catalogue of Brian's works at the book's conclusion, compiled by Lewis Foreman, is well set out and is the most complete in print (as it includes about 100 songs), although it is not free from error.

In the preface to *Ordeal by Music*, Nettel noted that he had had from Granville Bantock "the loan of his collection of Brian's letters going back some forty years".[8] Thus it is likely that he knew a great deal which he did not reveal in both biographies, in deference to Brian (who was alive as a preliminary version of the later one was being completed) and to his relatives and friends. Things missing from Nettel, particularly from the decade 1909-18, form the basis of Kenneth Eastaugh's book. It is essentially a vast exploration of the contents of the letters to Bantock and to a lesser extent of letters from Brian to Robert Simpson. But Eastaugh does a great deal more than quote from and relate what is in these letters. He creates a picture of Brian that is both more and less complete than any other to have appeared: more complete because much important material which Nettel did not deal with is brought out, and less complete because the chiefly negative aspects of Brian's character which he reveals are often allowed to stand for the whole person.

Eastaugh's aim was to correct publicly held views about Brian, especially the one that he did not care whether his music was performed, and also the one that Brian's misfortunes were never his fault. In successfully correcting these, he has implied a hypothesis that the personal crisis involving the breakup of Brian's first marriage and many events related to it shaped in some way his later creative output, that the struggle to prove himself musically grew out of the failures of his personal life. He may have a point, but it is too easy to accept this hypothesis because of its connection to the commonly held popular notion of the idealistic artist being totally unable to manage in the real world. It involves complex psychological and social issues which Eastaugh does not go into, for his book is basically a ground-breaker, not a building-finisher.

The ground he breaks covers a lot of territory indeed. A substantial amount of information provided is new, important, well presented, and a rich source for future research. Particularly valuable is the presentation of Brian's family background, and his activities up to about 1909. At that point the narrative concentrates almost exclusively on Brian's excesses and weaknesses for over 150 pages, and the making of points about Brian's character becomes repetitive and occasionally sensational.

The many and sometimes long extracts from Brian's cor-

respondence show him to be a brilliant writer of letters. A se-
lection of these — both the flamboyant earlier letters and the
laconic later ones — and of his many journal articles could
form the basis of a most welcome book. Brian had many critical insights lacking in his contemporaries, yet his writings
have not attracted much attention so far. There are many
paths to explore also in the connections between his literary
and musical endeavours.

Eastaugh includes a great many dates and places in his ex-
position, sometimes too many, but his procedure in this regard
is a welcome contrast to Nettel's. Nonetheless, some important quotations go undated, and his jumping around chronologically in the telling of the story, as necessary as it often
seems, adds to confusion about his written sources. His most
important oral sources were probably Brian's widow and
members of both his families. Unfortunately he is inclined to
consider them as reliable as written records. In general, there
is no more reason to approve the family members' testimony
in the 1970's about fine details of sensitive events occurring
many decades before than there is to take at face value Brian's
own statements from his last years, many of which Eastaugh
rightly shows to be unreliable. Eastaugh does rely on Brian,
however, on several points where he should not. One is the
timing of *Prometheus Unbound* (Brian's timings can be
erratic). Another is that "Bach never troubled whether *his*
works would be performed"[9] (this is a romanticized, rather
misleading exaggeration of Brian's).

Comparing supposedly identical quotations in Nettel's and
Eastaugh's books reveals important discrepancies. Words are
omitted, inserted, substituted, and rearranged without marking or comment. Authors ought to know better. Of course,
without the original documents in hand, little more can be
said about these authors' faithfulness to the sources. However,
in his book, Eastaugh misreads words in a letter from Brian's
patron Herbert Robinson to Brian which is given in facsimile
among the illustrations. Eastaugh's transcription of it is on
pp. 213-14. He is forced to add punctuation to the original to
get quasi-grammatical sense out of his misreading. Such things
do not inspire confidence in the author's ability to handle his
sources.

Brian's *Gothic Symphony* has received more attention than any other of his works, but its dates of composition are still uncertain. Sketches have not survived, and there are apparently no legible dates on the existing manuscripts. The final, oversize manuscript of the *Te Deum*, which is the last of the two parts of the symphony, is lost. The published score of the whole symphony carries only a copyright date. The main evidence about dates comes from Brian's letters, his oral statements, and one or two articles. Prior to Eastaugh's book, the accepted idea was that the symphony was begun in 1919, that the whole, consisting of a three-movement orchestral Part I and the choral-orchestral *Te Deum* Part II, was completed in a significant but not final form in 1922, and that Brian did not finish the final copy of the *Te Deum* (the one that is lost) until 1927. Eastaugh suggests that real work "in any depth" on *The Gothic* did not start until 1922, that Part I was completed in November 1924, and that the *Te Deum*, while possibly existing in some preliminary form before 1925, was not worked on "seriously" or as a part of the symphony until then.

He may be right, but the evidence for these conclusions is not presented convincingly in the book. Despite noting errors of various kinds in Brian's letters to Bantock, he takes Brian's references to *The Gothic* in these letters as literally as possible. And despite that, he does not try to determine what Brian may have meant in contexts related to *The Gothic* by such terms as *sketch, full score, scoring, fully sketched*, and *finished*. It is possible, of course, that Brian used some terms inconsistently. Furthermore, the explanation of Brian's working methods which Eastaugh offers (p. 229) resembles what he is believed to have done in broad outline for some much later works. It can not be taken as automatically valid for earlier ones such as *The Tigers* or *The Gothic*, considering the absence of so much manuscript material. A close examination of what Eastaugh reveals of the Bantock correspondence does not, in fact, rule out the *possibility* that both parts of the symphony were completed in all but final form long before the winter of 1924-25. Most importantly, he gives insufficient substantiation for November 1924 as the completion date of Part I. There are no footnotes in the book, so it is impossible to tell how he arrives at his conclusions and whether there is more evidence on these matters in the letters to Bantock.

There may be internal musical evidence to consider in a number of short works Brian may have sketched or completed as preparation for *The Gothic*, but this is beyond the scope of Eastaugh's book. Nonetheless, he does not even mention their existence. Some short completed works (piano music and songs) have dates of 1924 and 1925.[10] If these dates are correct, and if these works were studies for *The Gothic*, particularly for the *Te Deum* (both questions are far from resolved), then this would indeed support Eastaugh's suggestion that the *Te Deum* was not completed by and perhaps not started by 1925. Apart from the dating problem itself, Eastaugh may be right in suggesting there was a time in the 1920's when Brian considered the symphony complete with only three movements. In this form the work might not have had the designation *Gothic* attached to it. Eastaugh says nothing on this possibility, but none of his quotations from the winter of 1924-25 uses any title in reference to the work.

The best expositions on the music of the *Gothic Symphony* are the chapter in MacDonald's book reviewed earlier and a longer analysis in my own *Havergal Brian and His Symphony "The Gothic".*[11] The former owes a certain amount to the latter, which was completed before it, but the two studies were carried on for the most part independently. Many inspirations and influences have been mentioned for *The Gothic*, some by Brian himself. One of the most intriguing is gothic cathedral architecture in Britain: indeed, one of Brian's early, very vivid musical experiences was singing in Lichfield Cathedral, where he was attracted, curiously enough, to a *Te Deum* by Prince Albert. It is mainly from the architectural reference to *gothic* that the symphony takes its name, according to Brian, although he also explained the title in expanded senses, relating it to general characteristics of medieval life.[12] Many writers have mentioned the architectural meaning as connected to the symphony. MacDonald, for example, after doing so, calls the symphony "a great cathedral in sound".[13] But even he did not suspect then the odd truth lurking behind that concise label.

What follows is not a basic analysis or even description of

the *Gothic Symphony*. As mentioned, those can be found elsewhere. This is a speculative analysis, intended to show how the work can be heard in a musical equivalent to a gothic cathedral design. The wording here is important: no claim is made that Brian planned the parallels that are revealed between architecture and music, although some of the simpler and more general details he was probably aware of in a creative, rather than rational or analytical sense. The analysis merely provides an added dimension to the symphony's appreciation.

The most obvious general similarity between the symphony and gothic cathedrals is the monumental aspect. Cathedrals are indeed massive in size and weight, but that weight is not felt as great density. It is dispersed. Thickness of walls is disguised, the volume of structural supports is concealed, and massiveness is generally underemphasized. So too in Brian's symphony. It is long, about 99 minutes in the 1966 performance, and big, requiring an orchestra of about 200 players, three major vocal soloists (the solo alto has noticeably less music than the solo soprano, tenor, and bass), a children's chorus, and a very large double chorus. Yet colossal noises are rare in it. Its large dimensions seem to be used in order to employ a wide range of musical timbres and styles. And just as the force of a cathedral was offset by a multitude of basically linear ribs, shafts, buttresses, etc., so the force of the symphony, even in many climaxes, is offset by the counterpoint of many linear melodic shapes. Paradoxically, the profusion and intricacy of the writing at times reinforce the grandeur of the music because the individual details are less important than the resultant effect. A great deal of gothic ornamentation functions similarly.

Many sets of gothic ornaments contain items by separate craftsmen which are considered copies but which resemble each other in some but not all details. So also in the symphony, there are families of themes whose members are elusively related by varying melodic characteristics. Structural parallelism and balance do not entail close similarity.

For both religious and practical reasons, the cathedral's visual thrust is upward. The towers and spires, vaults and arches, play of light, and much ornamentation are directed towards this end. In the symphony, a great many themes, some quite long, move upwards, spreading sometimes through many octaves (e.g. ex. 1, which is half of a theme that ultimately reaches the D three and a half octaves above the opening A). Climaxes frequently use rising parallel progressions. If there is anything equivalent to the gothic arch in the music, it is the augmented triad. Several long passages and striking climaxes are built on such chords.

No work of Brian's extant, preceding or following, is as eclectic as *The Gothic*, particularly its Part II. There are many styles of writing in it, chronologically from medieval plainchant to 20th-century atonality. Critics who seize upon this as a weakness miss the point. MacDonald is quite right in noting that "the finale's [i.e. Part II's] encyclopaedic nature is an inevitable outcome of its exploratoriness. The immense structure seems to ransack the whole tradition of Western Music in search of a way forward."[14] Historical stylistic purity as an ideal is a post-medieval concept that is foreign to the *Gothic Symphony*, as it is to a lot of post-world-war II music. Nor was it an ideal to generations of people who rebuilt and expanded existing cathedrals. Even at the Reformation, by far the majority of British cathedrals showed mixed styles, if one accepts most of the traditional architectural categories of periodization.[15]

Throughout his life Brian was fascinated by cathedrals, chiefly but not exclusively English specimens. Frequently he noted that although the English gothic cathedrals differed greatly from each other, nearly all of them had the same basic plan. That basic plan is the crucifix.[16] It is also the basic plan of the *Gothic Symphony*: see ex. 2. The Roman numerals designate the movement numbers, i to iii being Part I of the symphony and iv to vi Part II (the *Te Deum*). The Arabic numerals represent the approximate timings of the movements in the B.B.C. performance of 30 October 1966, in order: 11 minutes, 10½, 12, 17½, 14, 34.[17] The diagram is drawn to scale according to these dimensions. The result is not a "perfect" crucifix, but the shape is clear, and much more so than many cathedral ground plans. A different performance might produce different timings, but the basic shape would remain.

The basic tonality of Part I is D, of Part II E. Hence the

horizontal axis is labelled D and the vertical axis E. However, the importance of E and keys closely allied to it increases within Part I as it progresses. One might note especially two important large-scale progressions in the second movement to be discussed shortly, and in the third movement pp. 70-72, centring around E, and pp. 91-99, centring around C#, which is very closely associated with E throughout the symphony.

The importance of D and its closely allied keys *decreases* within Part II as *it* progresses, and radically so after the fifth movement. These two tendencies (the increase of E in Part I, the decrease of D in Part II) are represented in ex. 2 by the parenthetical arrows: D "influences" the earlier parts of Part II as E does the later parts of Part I. More concisely, the domain of D is the top and the left of the diagram, and that of E is the bottom and right: see ex. 3. The only two unmixed quadrants in this example are the top-left and the bottom-right, hence the dotted D and E and the dotted oblique line in ex. 2. That line in ex. 2 reflects this most general division of domains.

The resultant suggested pairing of movements 1 and 4 and of movements 3 and 6 (each pair being on one side of the dotted line in ex. 2) is valid *apart* from large-scale tonal considerations. Both Part I and Part II progress individually from simpler and more traditionally oriented music to bolder, more varied, more nonthematic, more dramatic music. In this regard, movements 1 and 4 act as "bases" for the more complex, even bizarre music of movements 3 and 6 respectively.

The central movements 2 and 5 lie somewhere between the extremes in these matters. Tonally they each reveal a concentration on a "midpoint" between D and E. In the second movement, this is the melodic midpoint D# or E♭; in the fifth movement, it is the harmonic midpoint A on the circle of fifths, since A lies a perfect fifth below E and a perfect fifth above D.

The second movement is set in a joint tonality F# major/ D# minor. This pairing of two keys using the same basic set of pitch classes but different tonics is common in *The Gothic*. Furthermore, near the centre of the movement, the main theme heard in D minor[18] (it begins as ex. 4) gives way to a statement of different material suggesting E♭ minor, which is in turn followed by a restatement of this different material suggesting E minor. The later resumption of the main theme material of ex. 4 after a big climax is in E^b minor. *This* is then followed by a restatement of the main theme in E minor. The whole double progression is set out in ex. 5. On two different levels, the symphony's main tonal progression of D to E is filled in by D$^\#$/E^b to give D - D$^\#$ - E.

The fifth movement does not have as obvious an emphasis on A as the second does on D$^\#$. Yet the A minor triad is one of the four component triads in the movement's celebrated polyharmonic opening, the others being D minor, E minor, and G major. Keys of A also figure in the only two solo parts in the very difficult and complex *a cappella* section which begins the movement. The two solos are dramatic lines for the soprano. The first one (ex. 6) suggests a centre (hardly a key) of A; the second one (its beginning is shown in ex. 7) takes over on A from the *fortissimo* A major choral ending of the preceding passage. By the end (not shown) of the second solo, a key of E is strongly implied. The movement began in D. While it would be exaggerating to declare that the overall progression of this *a cappella* section is D - A - E, there are suggestions of it.

Yet another possible suggestion of A takes place later in the movement after an orchestral climax on the same augmented chord (C - E - G$^\#$) as is found in ex. 6. One might expect A to follow because of the earlier example. But instead, there follow four similar passages which begin on keys of (in order) F, G, B^b, and C. The sequence recalls the relationship to A by skipping over the key of A.

The key of A is significant on large levels in the other movements of Part II. Its relation to D is made clear in the fourth movement by a sombre *a cappella* A minor passage (pp. 139-40) framed by jubilant music in D Major and F$^\#$ major. A's relation to E emerges in the sixth movement through an A minor unison march for the clarinet family and drums (pp. 225 and 246) *framing* jubilant music substantially in E major.

There is a final group of possible parallels between the cruciform plan and the *Gothic Symphony*, returning to connections with cathedrals, especially English cathedrals. Although there does not seem to be a parallel between the idea of transepts and Part I, there are possible references to the choir arm and nave in Part II. Except for a relatively brief appearance of tenor and bass soloists in the *a cappella* opening section of the fourth movement, the singers in that section are all females and children. Could this be an equivalent to the lady chapel, found at the east end of the choir arm, i.e. the top of the diagram in ex. 2?

Towards the crossing of the two axes of the diagram, one comes to the holiest part of the cathedral, the sanctuary, and to the choir proper, part of which was indeed for choristers. Equivalent places in the music could be the *a cappella* sections in the fourth movement beginning on p. 128 and p. 139, and the *a cappella* opening section of the fifth movement. All three sections, especially the last-mentioned, contain elaborate and difficult choral music and possibly the most profound in the symphony as well.

The long sixth movement parallels the long nave of most English cathedrals. The nave was generally used by the laity. The sixth movement's emphasis on the male voices, both solo and choral, might symbolize that.[19] And just as the nave came to hold an astonishing variety of secular events,[20] so the sixth movement contains the greatest variety by far of secular music, including arias, marches, playing with the sounds of words, and glorious celebrations. Both the nave and the sixth movement ultimately derive their character and importance from the sometimes bizarre mixture of the sacred and the secular.

The centre of the crucifix in ex. 2 represents both the second and the fifth movements. The second is a massive funeral march and the fifth is a visionary treatment of the revelation implied in the only line of text used: *Judex crederis esse venturus*, literally "You are believed to be coming as (our) judge". Thus both movements deal with death, suggesting an equivalent to the crypt, which was originally under the sanctuary or near the crossing of the two axes, and which developed its functions from that of the place of rest of the sanctified dead.

Finally, the central tower/spire formations above the crossing of the axes and the two tower/spire formations at the west end of the nave (bottom of ex. 2)[21] might be considered represented by the four extra brass bands, no parts of which are used in Part I of the symphony, nor in the fourth movement, nor in the first three-fifths of the sixth. More particulary, one might note the highly dramatic passages for brass and/or percussion which the extra bands particpate in: *one* such passage in the fifth movement (p. 153) and *two towards the end of the sixth* (pp. 253-55 and 256-57).[22]

Further specific analogies might be found, but doubtless this has been carried far enough for now. More generally, the cathedral was considered by its religious users to be not merely a symbol, but the revelation itself of celestial vision and truth that transcended human existence. Brian was not religious, and the *Gothic Symphony* may or may not be constructed deliberately on a cathedral cruciform plan, but it may be that this composition adopted a similar significance for him. Work on it in the 1920's seems to have sustained him when little else did. It may have become more than a symbol or a substitute for reality — something closer to reality itself.

Footnotes to Chapter IV

1   Havergal Brian: "Values", in *Musical Opinion*, Mar. 1923, p. 540.

2   See the bibliography in this chapter for complete references for these books.

3   Its current address is: 33 Coopers Road, Little Heath, Potters Bar, Hertfordshire.

4   Letters to Walter Allum, also very important, came to light shortly after Brian's death. Eastaugh does not mention them, but Reginald Nettel does in *his* book, which is also reviewed later in the chapter.

5   Malcolm MacDonald: *The Symphonies of Havergal Brian* Volume 1; p. 10.

6   *Ibid.*; pp. 181-82.

7   Lewis Foreman: *Havergal Brian and the Performance of His Orchestral Music—A History and Sourcebook*; p. 11.

8   Reginald Nettel: *Ordeal by Music—The Strange Experience of Havergal Brian* (London: Oxford University Press, 1945); p. vi.

9   Kenneth Eastaugh: *Havergal Brian—The Making of a Composer*; p. 99.

10 Three piano works were published with the date of composition as 1924. On 30 September 1972, Graham Hatton drew up a list of manuscripts which Brian had recently sent to him. This list included several choral songs with dates of June 1925.

11 Paul Rapoport: *Havergal Brian and His Symphony "The Gothic"* (Ann Arbor, Michigan, U.S.A.: University Microfilms, 1972).

12 *Ibid.*; p. 188.

13 Malcolm MacDonald: *The Symphonies . . .* ; p. 21.

14 Malcolm MacDonald: *Havergal Brian—Perspective on the Music* (London: Triad Press, 1972); p. 29.

15 See Alec Clifton-Taylor: *The Cathedrals of England* (London: Thames and Hudson, 1967); especially pp. 15-16.

16 Brian did not specify the crucifix when he mentioned to me the idea of there being a basic plan for the cathedrals, in an interview on 15 July 1971; but he did in a letter to Franklyn Muench of 19 January 1969.

17 From here on in this chapter, Part II of the symphony, sometimes called the fourth movement, is subdivided as movements 4, 5, and 6. The music and the published score clearly suggest this division. There are other printed references to the timings of the movements which are incorrect.

18 Some of the modes mentioned in this paragraph might more accurately be described as minor/dorian.

19 especially the male *a cappella* passage setting *Salvum fac populum tuum, Domine*, literally "Preserve your people, (O) Lord". In any case, the third section of the *Te Deum* (i.e. the sixth movement of the symphony) is the only one to refer to "the people" directly.

20 See G.H. Cook: *The English Cathedral through the Centuries* (London: Phoenix House, 1957). Cook notes that because of activities carried on in the nave of Old St. Paul's Cathedral, an act was passed in 1554 forbidding people "to lead horses or mules or to carry casks of beer or loads of fruit or fish through the cathedral" (p. 36).

21 Lichfield Cathedral, which impressed Brian in his youth, is renowned for its central spire and western pair of spires.

22 The two passages towards the end of the sixth movement also use the organ, and the second of them has the E^b clarinets doubling the E^b cornets.

Allegro assai

Ex. 1: The Gothic (p. 3, m.4 to p. 4, m.4)

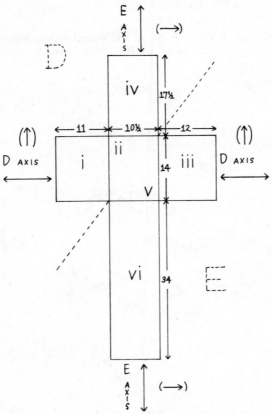

Ex. 2: The Gothic (in the B.B.C. performance)

D	D+E
D+E	E

Ex. 3: The Gothic (tonal domains)

Like a solemn march
hrp, strs

ff

Ex. 4: The Gothic (p. 48, mm. 4-5)

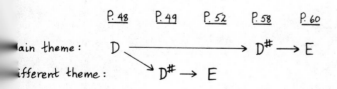

	P. 48	P. 49	P. 52	P. 58	P. 60

Main theme: D ⟶ D♯ ⟶ E

Different theme: D♯ ⟶ E

Ex. 5: The Gothic (2nd movement: 2 important progressions)

[Adagio]

Ex. 6: The Gothic (p. 149, mm. 21-27)

[Moderato]

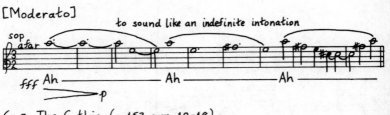

Ex. 7: The Gothic (p. 153, mm. 10-18)

ORCHESTRAL WORKS BY HAVERGAL BRIAN

For an explanation of abbreviations and what is included in this list, see page 19.

ENGLISH SUITE NO. 1 (1899, 1903-04? 1906?)
1st prf: 12.I.1907. Havergal Brian, Leeds Municipal Orc.
Pbd: Leipzig. Breitkopf & Härtel, 1914.

PSALM 23* (1901? 1905? full score lost ca. 1920, reconstructed 1945)
1st prf: 10.III.1973. László Heltay, cdr.; Leicestershire
            Schools S.O.; Brighton Festival Chorus; University of
            Sussex Choir; Stuart Holland, tenor.
Pbd: Chelmsford. Musica Viva, 1974 (vocal score only).

BURLESQUE VARIATIONS AND OVERTURE ON AN ORIGINAL
THEME (1903)

FOR VALOUR (1904, rev. 1906)
1st prf: 8.X.1907. Henry Wood, Queen's Hall Orc.
Pbd: Leipzig. Breitkopf & Härtel, 1914.

HERO AND LEANDER (1904-05? full score and parts lost)
1st prf: 3.XII.1908. Thomas Beecham, New S.O.

BY THE WATERS OF BABYLON (1905, rev. 1909; full score and
            parts lost)
1st prf: 18.IV.1907. Havergal Brian, cdr.; Staffordshire
            Orchestral Society; North Staffordshire District
            Choral Society; Frederic Austin, baritone.
Pbd: London. Breitkopf & Härtel, 1907 (vocal score only).

THE VISION OF CLEOPATRA (1907; full score and parts lost)
1st prf: 14.X.1909. Landon Ronald, cdr.; Hallé Orc.; South-
            port Festival Chorus; Maud Phillips, soprano; Lily
            Whiteside, mezzo-soprano; Phyllis Lett, alto; John
            Coates, tenor.
Pbd: London. Bosworth, 1909 (vocal score only).

FANTASTIC SYMPHONY (1907-08, rev. 1912; two movements remain
            (the next two items in this list) and any others are
            lost)

FANTASTIC VARIATIONS ON AN OLD RHYME (see note for
            Fantastic Symphony)
1st prf: 23.IV.1921. Henry Lyell-Tayler, [Brighton] West
            Pier Orc.
Pbd: Leipzig. Breitkopf & Härtel, 1914.

FESTAL DANCE (see note for *Fantastic Symphony*)
1st prf: 14.XII.1914. Granville Bantock, Midland Institute
               School of Music Orc.
Pbd: Leipzig. Breitkopf & Härtel, 1914.

IN MEMORIAM (1910)
1st prf: 26.XII.1921. Landon Ronald, Scottish Orc.
Pbd: Leipzig. Brietkopf & Härtel, 1913.

DOCTOR MERRYHEART (*Comedy Overture No. 1*) (1911-12)
1st prf: 3.I.1913. Julius Harrison, Musical League and Incor-
               porated Society of Musicians Festival Orc.
Pbd: Leipzig. Breitkopf & Härtel, 1913.

ENGLISH SUITE NO. 3 (1919, 21)
1st prf: 16.III.1922. Dan Godfrey, Bournemouth Municipal
               Orc.

SYMPHONY NO. 1, *The Gothic** (1919-27?)
1st prf: 24.VI.1961. Bryan Fairfax, cdr.; Polyphonia Orc.;
               Royal Military School of Music; London Philharmonic
               Choir; Kingsway Choral Society; London Orpheus
               Choir; Hendon Grammar School Choir; Noelle Barker,
               soprano; Jean Evans, alto; Kenneth Bowen, tenor;
               John Shirley-Quirk, bass.
Pbd: London. Cranz, 1932 (reprinted 1976).

ENGLISH SUITE NO. 4, *Kindergarten* (1921? 1924?)
1st prf: 5.VII.1977. Martin Rutherford, First Orc. of George
               Heriot's School.

SYMPHONY NO. 2 (1930-31)
1st prf: 19.V.1973. Leslie Head, Kensington S.O.
Pbd: Chelmsford. Musica Viva, 1973.

SYMPHONY NO. 3 (1931-32)
1st prf: 18.X.1974. Stanley Pope, New Philharmonia Orc.

SYMPHONY NO. 4, *Das Siegeslied* (1932-33)
1st prf: 3.VII.1967. Maurice Handford, cdr.; B.B.C. Northern
               S.O.; Halifax Choral Society; Leeds Philharmonic
               Choir; Honor Sheppard, soprano.

SYMPHONY NO. 5, *Wine of Summer* (1937)
1st prf: 11.XII.1969. Leslie Head, cdr.; Kensington S.O.
               Brian Rayner Cook, baritone.

PROMETHEUS UNBOUND (1937-44; full score lost)
Note: for soloists, chorus, and orchestra.

SYMPHONY NO. 6, *Sinfonia Tragica** (1947-48)
  1st prf: 21.IX.1966. Douglas Robinson, Orc. of the Royal
                  Opera House, Covent Garden.

THE TINKER'S WEDDING (*Comedy Overture No. 2*) (1948)
  1st prf: 25.VI.1950. Eric Warr, B.B.C. Scottish S.O.

SYMPHONY NO. 7 (1948)
  1st prf: 13.III.1968. Harry Newstone, Royal P.O.

SYMPHONY NO. 8* (1949)
  1st prf: 1.II.1954. Adrian Boult, London P.O.
  Pbd: Chelmsford. Musica Viva, 1973.

SYMPHONY NO. 9* (1951)
  1st prf: 22.III.1958. Norman del Mar, B.B.C. S.O.

ENGLISH SUITE NO. 5, *Rustic Scenes** (1953)
  1st prf: Gramophone record CBS 61612, issued February
                  1975. Eric Pinkett, Leicestershire Schools S.O.

SYMPHONY NO. 10* (1953-54)
  1st prf: 3.XI.1958. Stanley Pope, Philharmonia Orc.
  Pbd: Chelmsford. Musica Viva, 1973.

SYMPHONY NO. 11 (1954)
  1st prf: 5.XI.1959. Harry Newstone, London S.O.

ELEGY (1954)
  1st prf: 17.II.1977. Brian Wright, Guildhall School of Music
                  and Drama S.O.

SYMPHONY NO. 12* (1957)
  1st prf: 5.XI.1959. Harry Newstone, London S.O.

SYMPHONY NO. 13 (1959)

SYMPHONY NO. 14* (1959-60)
  1st prf: 10.V.1970. Edward Downes, London S.O.

SYMPHONY NO. 15 (1960)

SYMPHONY NO. 16* (1960)
  1st prf: Gramophone record Lyrita SRCS.67, issued May
                  1975. Myer Fredman, London P.O.

SYMPHONY NO. 17 (1960-61)

SYMPHONY NO. 18 (1961)
  1st prf: 26.II.1962. Bryan Fairfax, Polyphonia Orc.

SYMPHONY NO. 19 (1961)
1st prf: 31.XII.1976. John Canarina, B.B.C. Scottish S.O.

THE JOLLY MILLER (*Comedy Overture No. 3*) (1962)
1st prf: 15.XI.1974. Robert Fitzpatrick, Main Line S.O., in
              Philadelphia, Pennsylvania, U.S.A.

SYMPHONY NO. 20 (1962)
1st prf: 5.X.1976. Vernon Handley, New Philharmonia Orc.

SYMPHONY NO. 21* (1963)
1st prf: 10.V.1970. Edward Downes, London S.O.
Pbd: Chelmsford. Musica Viva, 1973.

CONCERTO FOR ORCHESTRA (1964)
1st prf: 12.IV.1975. Joseph Stones, Leeds College of Music
              S.O.

SYMPHONY NO. 22, *Symphonia Brevis** (1964-65)
1st prf: 15.VIII.1971. Myer Fredman, Royal P.O.
Pbd: Chelmsford. Musica Viva, 1977.

SYMPHONY NO. 23* (1965)
1st prf: 4.X.1973. Bernard Goodman, University of Illinois
              S.O.

SYMPHONY NO. 24 (1965)
1st prf: 18.VI.1975. Myer Fredman, London P.O.

SYMPHONY NO. 25 (1965-66)
1st prf: 31.XII.1976. John Canarina, B.B.C. Scottish S.O.

SYMPHONY NO. 26 (1966)
1st prf: 13.V.1976. Nicholas Smith, North Staffordshire S.O.

SYMPHONY NO. 27 (1966-67)

SYMPHONY NO. 28* (1967)
1st prf: 5.X.1973. Leopold Stokowski, New Philharmonia
              Orc.

SYMPHONY NO. 29 (1967)
1st prf: 17.XI.1976. Nicholas Smith, North Staffordshire S.O.

SYMPHONY NO. 30 (1967)
1st prf: 24.IX.1976. Harry Newstone, New Philharmonia Orc.

SYMPHONY NO. 31 (1968)

LEGEND FOR ORCHESTRA: AVE ATQUE VALE (1968)

SYMPHONY NO. 32 (1968)
    1st prf: 28.I.1971. Leslie Head, Kensington S.O.

OTHER WORKS

two concertos for violin and orchestra (1934, 1934-35), one for cello
and orchestra (1964); five operas: *The Grotesques* (renamed *The Tigers*)
(1916-30?), *Turandot* (1950-51), *The Cenci* (1952), *Faust* (1955-56),
Agamemnon (1957); *Legend* for violin and piano (1919?); six works for
piano; over 100 songs. Many works, orchestral and other, are lost. The
four most important lost full scores are probably those to *By the Waters
of Babylon*, *The Vision of Cleopatra*, *The Tigers*, and *Prometheus Unbound*.

DISCOGRAPHY OF ORCHESTRAL WORKS IN THE MAIN LIST

PSALM 23. László Heltay, cdr.; Leicestershire Schools S.O.; Brighton
    Festival Chorus; Paul Taylor, tenor. CBS 61612 (with Brian: English
    Suite No. 5 and Symphony No. 22).

SYMPHONY NO. 1, *The Gothic*. Adrian Boult, cdr.; B.B.C. S.O.; B.B.C.
    Chorus; B.B.C. Choral Society; City of London Choir; Hampstead
    Choral Society; Choir of Emanuel School; Orpington Junior Singers;
    Honor Sheppard, soprano; Shirley Minty, alto; Ronald Dowd, tenor;
    Roger Stalman, bass. Aries LP-2601 (pirated records listing no per-
    formers except Boult).

SYMPHONY NO. 6, *Sinfonia Tragica*. Myer Fredman, London P.O.
    a) Lyrita SRCS.67; b) Musical Heritage Society MHS 3426 (both
    with Brian: Symphony No. 16).

SYMPHONY NO. 8. Myer Fredman, Royal P.O. Aries LP-1603 (with
    Brian: Symphony No. 14 — pirated record listing fictitious per-
    formers).

SYMPHONY NO. 9. Myer Fredman, Royal P.O. Aries LP-1604 (with
    Brian: Symphony No. 12 and No. 23 — pirated record listing ficti-
    tious performers).

ENGLISH SUITE NO. 5, *Rustic Scenes*. Eric Pinkett, Leicestershire
    Schools S.O. CBS 61612 (with Brian: Psalm 23 and Symphony No.
    22).

SYMPHONY NO. 10. James Loughran, Leicestershire Schools S.O.
    Unicorn RHS 313 (with Brian: Symphony No. 21).

SYMPHONY NO. 12. Norman del Mar, B.B.C. S.O. Aries LP-1604
    (with Brian: Symphony No. 9 and No. 23 — pirated record listing
    fictitious performers).

SYMPHONY NO. 14. Edward Downes, London S.O. Aries LP-1603 (with Brian: Symphony No. 8 — pirated record listing fictitious performers).

SYMPHONY NO. 16. Myer Fredman, London P.O. a) Lyrita SRCS. 67; b) Musical Heritage Society MHS 3426 (both with Brian: Symphony No. 6).

SYMPHONY NO. 21. Eric Pinkett, Leicestershire Schools S.O. Unicorn RHS 313 (with Brian: Symphony No. 10).

SYMPHONY NO. 22, *Symphonia Brevis*. László Heltay, Leicestershire Schools S.O. CBS 61612 (with Brian: Psalm 23 and English Suite No. 5).

SYMPHONY NO. 23. Bernard Goodman, University of Illinois S.O. Aries LP-1604 (with Brian: Symphony No. 9 and No. 12 — pirated record listing fictitious performers).

SYMPHONY NO. 28. Leopold Stokowski, New Philharmonia Orc. Aries LP-1607 (with Brian: Concerto for Violin and Orchestra No. 2 (Stanley Pope, cdr.; New Philharmonia Orc.; Ralph Holmes, violin) — pirated record listing fictitious performers).

ORCHESTRAL AUTOGRAPH MANUSCRIPTS

Most of those extant are with the family of one of the composer's children. Enquiries should be addressed to Brian's publisher Musica Viva (U.K.).

SELECTED WRITINGS BY HAVERGAL BRIAN

Note: Every month from September 1931 to June 1940, the journal *Musical Opinion* carried a lead article-editorial titled "On the Other Hand, by La Main Gauche". It seems that Brian wrote by far most of the material appearing under that title, but it is probably impossible now to create a complete and accurate catalogue of his contributions. None of these is cited below.

"The first symphony of Arnold Bax", in *Musical Opinion*, Dec. 1922; pp. 253-54.

"Placing", in *Musical Opinion*, Feb. 1923; pp. 456-57.

"Values", in *Musical Opinion*, Mar. 1923; p. 540.

"The brass band", in *Musical Opinion*, Aug. 1923; pp. 1043-44—Nov. 1923; pp. 160-61.

"The art of Frederick Delius", in *Musical Opinion*, Mar. 1924; p. 598—Apr. 1924; pp. 700-01—May 1924; pp. 799-800—June 1924; pp. 906-

07—July 1924; pp. 1002-03—Aug. 1924; p. 1098—Sep. 1924; pp. 1194-95—Oct. 1924; pp. 49-50.

"Sir Henry J. Wood", in *Musical Opinion*, Aug. 1933; pp. 926-27.

"Arnold Schönberg", in *Musical Opinion*, Sep. 1937; pp. 1035-36.

"How the 'Gothic' Symphony came to be written", in *Modern Mystic*, Dec. 1938; pp. 478-82, 485.

"Between two wars", in *Musical Opinion*, Dec. 1941; pp. 81-82—Jan. 1942; pp. 120-21.

"The faraway years", in *Musical Opinion*, Jan. 1949; pp. 179, 181, 183.

SELECTED WRITINGS BY OTHERS ABOUT BRIAN

Reginald Nettel: *Ordeal by Music—The Strange Experience of Havergal Brian* (London: Oxford University Press, 1945).

Harold Truscott: "Havergal Brian", in Robert Simpson, ed.: *The Symphony* Volume 2, corrected edition (Harmondsworth: Penguin Books, 1969); pp. 140-52. Errors appearing in the Brian chapter in the first edition of 1967 were corrected for the next one of 1969.

Robert Simpson: "Brian's symphonies", in R.L.E. [i.e. Lewis] Foreman, ed.: *Havergal Brian—A Collection of Essays* (London: Triad Press, 1969); pp. 14-15.

Deryck Cooke: "Havergal Brian and his Gothic Symphony", in *The Musical Times*, no. 1484, vol. 107, Oct. 1966; pp. 859-63.

Malcolm MacDonald: *Havergal Brian—Perspective on the Music* (London: Triad Press, 1972).

Paul Rapoport: *Havergal Brian and His Symphony "The Gothic"* (Ann Arbor, Michigan, U.S.A.: University Microfilms, 1972). M. Mus. thesis for the University of Illinois at Urbana-Champaign [Illinois, U.S.A.] , 1972.

Malcolm MacDonald: *The Symphonies of Havergal Brian* Volume 1 (London: Kahn and Averill, 1974).

Lewis Foreman: *Havergal Brian and the Performance of His Orchestral Music—A History and Sourcebook* (London: Thames Publishing, 1976).

Reginald Nettel: *Havergal Brian and His Music* (London: Dennis Dobson, 1976).

Kenneth Eastaugh: *Havergal Brian—The Making of a Composer* (London: George C. Harrap, 1976).

Allan Pettersson in the early 1950's

V   Allan Pettersson and his Symphony No. 2

I am not a composer; I am a voice crying out, a voice crying out *(something that must not be forgotten) which threatens to be drowned in the noise of the times.*[1]

Many people, on reading statements of this sort by Allan Pettersson, may think he is a crank, or at least that his words must be an exaggeration. Few other composers have ever said things like this publicly.

> I feel I have more affinity with criminals, those who are called criminals, than with other people, not because of what is called their criminality, but because of their longing for freedom, their anguish and suffering, their *feeling of being outside.*[2]

> When I work I forget Pettersson, whom I am genuinely tired of. But there within the ribs is a meeting place, the heart's red place (sorry about the poetry!), where I meet all mankind, where everybody always is and where everybody is one.[3]

These and similar impassioned quotations admit proper perspective when one realizes that Pettersson does not have a private *and* a public mode of expression. For him they are nearly the same. He has always said and written what he has thought, undiluted and pretty well uncensored. The reason may be that all his communications are aimed at real persons, even if they are unknown to him. To read him correctly, one must assume the role of listener in a private conversation with him, not the role of reader of something remote translated by the printed medium. Pettersson is also a poet by nature: his articles and the interviews with him must often be

[1]   See footnotes p.122

understood as the creative productions of an intense artist, not as mere matter-of-fact reporting or as simple answers to simple questions. Pettersson himself realized one aspect of the problem when he wrote:

> "My material is my own life, the blessed, the damned," I once said. People in present times, in today's welfare society, may think that such language is dramatized overambition, and this very misjudgement reveals a lack of deeper insight into how a person was moulded in an environment of misery, in another society, which the current one admittedly developed out of. [4]

Pettersson was born on 19 September 1911 in Västra Ryd, Uppland, Sweden to working-class parents. His father was a smith with no real taste for music. His mother he remembers much more fondly. She was religious and often sang and played the guitar. Pettersson's youth was spent in a grim slum area of southern Stockholm; he lived mainly in a cellar with bars on the windows in crowded, unsanitary conditions, conditions of poverty and illness. He liked to read, especially philosophy and religion. Interest in music, however, soon came to dominate all else. He has told how he sold Christmas cards when very young so as to be able to buy a violin.

His playing of it may have been too frequent and too wild: neighbours thought it was and suggested to his mother that he be sent to a reformatory. He played the violin whenever he could, at political meetings, funerals, beerhalls, cinemas, amusement parks — alone or in combination with others (he recalls accordion, banjo, guitar, and drums).

In his teens he made two unsuccessful attempts to enter the Music Academy in Stockholm. Both times he was refused an audition. There may have been additional reasons, but Pettersson felt then that members of his low social class were not wanted at the academy. Humiliation was added to his other misfortunes.

> Perhaps [my music] is a protest against predestination, cruelty towards the individual, the individual without a chance. [5]

He finally gained admission to the academy in 1931, but he still felt he was an outsider. He had little money for his musical education and no piano at home for the constant keyboard work required. Accordingly, he tried to work at various places that did have pianos. In the fall of 1935, having been accustomed to using a piano in a room in a church, he was suddenly denied its use when the church's neighbours complained of the light coming from the church at night.[6] From around this time come Pettersson's first compositions, including six rather pessimistic songs from 1935.

At the conservatory he studied mainly violin, viola, theory, and composition. After many years of hard work he was awarded a Jenny Lind fellowship in 1939 to study abroad. He considered going to study in America with Hindemith, partly because he could then keep working at both viola and composition together. But it was decided he should go to France. He did go but returned to Stockholm quickly because of the war.

From 1940 to 1951, Pettersson was a violist in the Stockholm Concert Society Orchestra, which is now the Stockholm Philharmonic Orchestra.[7] He took his work very seriously, often practising during concert intervals and thus annoying his colleagues who preferred to be taking a break. During these years he also continued to work at composition, studying with Otto Olsson, Tor Mann, and Karl-Birger Blomdahl.

In 1943-45 he wrote many poems which he intended to set to music. The 24 he did set (out of perhaps 100) he called *Barefoot Songs*. Many of them probably have strong auto-biographical connections:

Mother Is Poor

Mother is poor and the pot sits empty,
and the cold is piercing and howls.
The boy is thin and squints,
and he arches his back like a cat.
Father is in good spirits with his schnapps;
he talks about stars and planets.
Yes, the Lord God has no interest
in the star that is called Earth.[8]

The poems are in simple, direct, often sparse language, drawing on Swedish folklore as well as their author's own life for their subjects. Like the poems in the 1935 set of songs (those texts were by various Swedish and Finnish poets, not Pettersson himself), these carry mostly pessimistic, depressing messages about alienating experiences befalling the helpless individual. The musical language has qualities similar to those of the literary one, but it adds dimensions and possibilities not readily apparent in the texts alone. Pettersson notes that he might have set many more of the poems to music, but the refusal of Swedish Radio and of Nordiska Musikförlaget to take interest in them may have put off the desire to do so.[9]

During most of his years as violist, his music was written in his spare time, and none of it was performed. Both these things bothered him. He was once offered the position of section leader in the orchestra but declined it, preferring to keep what extra time he had for his composing.

His first big composition was a Concerto for Violin and String Quartet (without orchestra), written in 1949. Blomdahl, remarking on technical aspects of the concerto, reportedly said "I wouldn't dare write like that", but there was probably some admiration in his statement. Members of Pettersson's orchestra were surprised to learn of the concerto: very few of them knew he was a composer. Even three years later, a member of a Swedish music jury doubted that a concerto for string orchestra, written by Pettersson in 1949-50, could be his, because he was only an orchestra player.[10]

Pettersson returned to Paris in autumn 1951 for further study that was to last until spring 1953. First he was in a class under Arthur Honegger, but for most of his time in Paris he was a private student of René Leibowitz. Again he worked very hard, chiefly at technical exercises, some of them in twelve-tone methods. But twelve-tone serialism has left few traces on his music. He appears to have treated these exercises merely as drill, useful in developing his compositional techniques in ways at most only incidentally related to serialism. Years later he offered the opinion that "I had my teachers in order to be able to say: now I know this stuff, but to hell with it."[11]

In Paris Pettersson continued to compose, in addition to doing the heavy load of composition-related studies with Leibowitz. At this time, he still preferred to work with a piano. This meant going to a Catholic church in the morning and the Swedish church in Paris in the afternoon or evening. In the latter he worked in a cellar with an inferior piano.

> It was a marvellous piano . . . It was so out of tune and harsh in sound. I was fond of that sound; it sang in a sort of human way.[12]

He finished his second symphony in Stockholm in 1953. It was performed the next year by Tor Mann, who also gave the first performance of three other large-scale works by Pettersson. To him goes credit for being aware of Pettersson's merit and doing something about it at that time.

During the next decade, Pettersson wrote five large works. Four of them were performed a year or two after they were finished; another had to wait twelve years. But he was not pleased with the attitude of those in musical power towards him, and with the lack of understanding his music received. He still felt very much an outsider, partly because of his class origins and his struggles, but also because his music was so unlike what was being written in Sweden at the time. Large-scale, tonal, expressionistic symphonies, definitely not neo-classical or serial, were what he was producing: many people may have considered them old-fashioned and not worth looking into past the surface. Furthermore, his independent position, irascible temperament, and highly charged mode of expressing himself verbally probably were abrasive and created much ill will among potential supporters. For the few performances of his works, he appeared for rehearsals and concerts, occasionally wrote an article or gave information to others for one, and then disappeared to continue composing.

For the first performance of his third concerto for string orchestra in 1958, Pettersson gave an interview to Urban Stenström. This interview contains a number of important statements of Pettersson's beliefs at the time, including a remarkable passionate outburst relating again to his youth:

> It is mother who *is* my music. It is her voice that speaks in it, I've wanted to cry out what she could never say, she and my sister, my sister who never got to be a woman, who was stunted by rheumatoid arthritis, who nearly threw herself out of the window because of the pain and who died one Christmas eve in the Söder Hospital.[13]

These living images became even more real as Pettersson himself contracted the disease. Shortly after the first performance of his fifth symphony, which took place in November 1963, the rheumatoid arthritis put him in a hospital, interfering with his work on the sixth symphony. The fifth was, in fact, the last work which he could write out himself in a fair copy easily usable by conductors.[14] Composing and writing became difficult, but he had always lived for music and was not going to give it up.

Stig Westerberg, who had been the conductor of the first performance of the fifth symphony, made the first two records of Pettersson's orchestral music, in the mid-1960's. However, Pettersson sees the real breakthrough in his attempts to reach a wider audience as having occurred with the performances of the seventh symphony under Antal Doráti. Not long after he had become conductor of the Stockholm Philharmonic (in 1967), Doráti saw by chance the score to Pettersson's seventh symphony and quickly decided to perform it. The last three months of 1968 produced a mini-festival of Pettersson's music in Sweden. The seventh symphony was first performed in October, on the same night as many of the *Barefoot Songs* were being given first performances. The second concerto for string orchestra was first heard (under Westerberg) on 1 December, and on six of the following seven days, all 24 *Barefoot Songs* were heard for the first time as a group, broadcast by Swedish Radio. Around this time, Pettersson was made an honorary member of the Philharmonic and Doráti decided to record the seventh and include it in foreign tour with the orchestra in 1969.

This rapid increase of interest in Pettersson in Sweden is reflected by the recording dates of the 15 different performances of his music on commercial records:[15] twelve of them are 1968 or later.

A different turning point, in the other direction, occurred in the summer of 1970 when Pettersson finished his ninth symphony. His chronic illness was causing very severe complications. He was finally forced to go to a hospital, where he led a precarious existence for most of the nine months he remained there. Nevertheless, he got ideas during that stay for two further symphonies, which he completed in the two years following his release from the hospital.

Asked in 1974 about the onset of his illness about ten years earlier, he said:

> [It] didn't really change my situation at all. I was already enclosed in my own world and had adjusted to the loner's struggle.[16]

For many years before the mid-1960's, Pettersson had as little as possible to do with the outside musical world. After that, his illness made him an invalid, a prisoner in his own dark flat, where he lived four storeys up with no lift in an old building in southern Stockholm. He may have liked the place in some ways, as it was part of the area he grew up in. Nonetheless, after nearly 20 years there, he and his wife accepted a change of residence in October 1976 to a much brighter, more splendid and more manageable residence. In the preceding years Pettersson had come to realize that others had a genuine interest in him as a person and a composer, and that many things were being done for him, including the setting up of the new residence by the government, not out of condescension but out of compassion and appreciation.

But he has always been incensed by what appear to be machinations going on behind his back in matters in which he feels he should have direct involvement. In late 1974, the Stockholm Philharmonic and its new conductor Gennadiy Rozhdestvenskiy were planning the orchestra's short 1975 American tour. Early indications had been that they might take Pettersson's seventh symphony with them, especially as Doráti's recording of it had received some very favourable American reviews. As time passed, it became clear that this would not happen, possibly because Rozhdestvenskiy did not like the work. When the tour programmes were announced in June 1975 and Pettersson's music was not on any, he responded by banning the orchestra from playing his music. The Stockholm press unfortunately made it look as if the ban resulted merely from his being omitted from the tour. But actually this omission was the last in a series of incidents which Pettersson saw as underhanded attempts to put him down. Several promises had been made by the orchestra which, as far as he could tell, were not being kept. The only way he found he could put an end to the musico-political intrigues and the decisions being made against him was to remove all matters of choice from anyone's hands but his own. Hence the ban, which he had no intention of lifting. But he did lift it a year later, after much-needed cooling off on all sides and some quiet negotiations conducted without the press as catalyst.

The nature of Pettersson's music is indicated by something he said in a nonmusical context:

> The price of rosy objectivity is the relinquishing of vital, primitive, life-expiating emotions and this leads to the only expressive being on Earth becoming emotionally empty, destitute. If things go that far, man's role is played out.[17]

His symphonies are expansive, highly emotional, anguished creations which owe nothing to the various objectively oriented artistic movements of the 20th century. Spiritually there is a connection to late Mahler and late Sibelius. There are many reminders of both in Pettersson's music, but this may be due as much to similarities of situation and attitude as to anything else. His music transcends whatever he learned from them; his musical world is both more restricted and more disturbing.

The most apparent unusual feature of the symphonies is length, not only of whole works but of movements and sections within them. Only the third and the eighth symphonies[18] have numbered movements with any pause between them; all the others play without pause. The shortest, no. 11, is about 24 minutes; the two longest are no. 6 (about 57 minutes) and no. 9 (about 82 minutes). Internal proportions are sometimes pushed to extremes: the ninth contains seven minutes of unrelieved torment based on chromatic scales and a driving ostinato rhythm (see ex. 1), and the sixth has a coda almost exclusively in B^b minor which is about 45% of the length of the entire work.

Literal repetition is an important aspect of these two sections, of the rest of the two symphonies, and of the others as well. It serves many functions, from the simple confirmation of a cadence, tonality, or mood, to the more complicated growth towards confrontation of apparently calm and stable elements with unstable, at times grotesque and barbaric forces.

In the three symphonies from the 1950's, an extended period of calm, diatonic melody in a simple texture, especially one in a major key, almost always brings "disturbances", ranging from a few chromatic inflections that weaken the tonal stability (see later ex. 8, from the Symphony No. 2) to a complete collapse of the serenity by a sudden attack from the full orchestra *fff* (a fine example occurs on pp. 128-37 of the Symphony No. 4).

In the symphonies nos. 5 to 9, there is a change in the opposition between wild, nontonal heterophony and melodious, tonal calm. The earlier symphonies, nos. 2 to 4, pit one against the other frequently, and the struggle seems to have no winner. The later ones, nos. 5 to 9, contain longer sections of each, with calm definitely being attained at the end. But it is not the calm of quiet victory or joy. It is the calm of despair and resignation. The next symphony, no. 10, ends with a loud climax in C# major, but even this is no gesture of confidence — rather one of defiance and grim, fiendish determination. Lars Sjöberg calls it a "dance in honour of life",[19] but it is more a dance against and in constant threat of death.

I could never have a symphony pour out into a jubilant, victorious fanfare as a tremendous *yea* to life. Because man *doesn't* win the struggle![20]

Pettersson's music, while by no means a description of his life and attitudes, reflects them strongly. The tenth symphony, for all its daunting vigour and force and its defiant ending, is essentially a tragic work, expressing the philosophy of the previous symphonies, even if marking a new stage in his compositions — by its very high density of activity throughout, among much else.

Pettersson wrote his Symphony No. 2 during the latter part of his study with Leibowitz and then in Stockholm on his return there. The end of his autograph manuscript states "Paris-Stockholm 1952-53". Pettersson also said he wrote the symphony "behind Leibowitz's back", presumably meaning concurrently with but quite independently of his studies with Leibowitz. Certainly there is no use of pitch serialism in this work, although there are similarities to "byproducts" of serial practice in such details as wide octave displacement, the dominance of the same interval class in both horizontal and vertical constructions, and the strongly expressionistic style. Nonetheless, considering the one publicly available orchestral work written before this symphony (the Concerto for String Orchestra No. 1), it is likely that Leibowitz's teaching at most reinforced existing tendencies in Pettersson's music but did not create radically new ones.

The Symphony No. 2 is in one long movement, about 40 minutes. It is a work of extreme tension and extreme contrasts, a work of unrest, grotesquerie, despair, turbulence, terror. To explain why these impressions are created is an elaborate and perhaps impossible task, yet a few features of the music can be pointed out which contribute to them.

One is the interval class of a minor second — and the two main melodic fragments of the symphony (exs. 2 and 3) which are built out of it. Both fragments are unstable in that they are not treated as fixed themes. Among other variabilities, ex. 2 is sometimes longer and frequently shorter (e.g. only the viola part), and the size of the seconds may vary; ex. 3 does not always sound such jagged rhythms or wide leaps. More importantly, there is no sense of statement versus development. Both fragments change constantly.

Despite transpositions of exs. 2 and 3, it is remarkable how often they are untransposed. The "reason" is that the whole symphony centres around the pitch classes B and C, and around that particular half-step interval class between them. Emphasis is also placed on B♭ and C♯ and the further half- and whole-steps (but not augmented seconds or minor thirds) created among the four pitch classes.

An early suggestion of the later conflict between B♭ and B occurs in the first 15 measures of the symphony. Over pedal Bs, a short rhythmic figure is introduced slowly and quietly on E, C, F, and then G. After a sudden cadence, the same figure recurs on E, C, and then G, but over pedal B♭s. The passage on B♭ sounds deliberately "wrong". This is the first juxtaposition of B♭ and B, which often "meet" in comparable passages in E♭ minor and E minor. An example of this also occurs in the work's introduction (so marked in Italian and consisting of five of the whole 40 minutes) through the use of ex. 4

on a chord of E minor; earlier it was heard in a similar shape a half-step lower on a chord of E^b minor.

The falling minor sixth of ex. 4 is a main item in this symphony. It is hardly a motive, as it undergoes no extensive treatment. It acts more like a symbol, pathetic in a literal sense, quietly producing or trying to produce calm in pure diatonic harmony, often in the midst of something that is anything but calm or diatonic.

As the symphony progresses, harmonic use of the half-step ideas becomes clearer and more dramatic. Several passages involving pitch classes B and C in the violins at the top of their range can be traced to ex. 3 (see ex. 5). Some other passages emphasizing half-steps are nonthematic and essentially nonmelodic. Three of these are especially notable (on pp. 65-66, 106, and 138) because they are almost static yet quite unstable: they are "sound worlds" of uniform texture, range, and timbre, yet nontonal and nonmetrical. Still other half-step-dominated passages are contrapuntally wild and ferocious, with rapid changes in several parameters.

A more obvious contributor to the instability in the symphony is the rapid and irregular changes of tempo. The introduction, for example, goes through a cycle of speeding up and slowing down four times in its 58 measures. Towards the end of the work there is a passage of about 40 measures (pp. 119-22) having about 20 changes of tempo, several of them sudden and extreme. In this passage, changes of dynamics are almost as unpredictable, and familiar themes and gestures become distorted as expectations for continuity are constantly thwarted. Ex. 6 illustrates some of these effects, with timbre and range relatively unchanging.[21] At the suggestion of regularity of irregularity in the example's fifth measure, this music is dropped. In the next measure something else begins, *vivace*.

Sudden changes in musical ideas may nevertheless involve some continuity. In the instance just mentioned, the C (ex. 6, m. 6) acts as a link to the music that precedes, the sound of the violins' G-string remains prominent, and the B^b-A recurs. This is but one of the many places where some aspects of a quite different gesture have an origin in what immediately precedes it.

Instability is also created by use of a gesture which has al-

most no connection to its immediate environment. Ex. 4
occasionally intrudes where it might least be expected. In ex.
7, it is in turn interrupted by an unprepared *ff* chord from
the whole orchestra. The interruption returns and expands
beginning in the last measure of ex. 7. It is another manifes-
tation of the B^b-B conflict, but locally it is heard as a severe
jolt in a passage marked, perhaps ironically, *molto tranquillo
con sentimento*.

A different kind of interruption occurs in some of the
most lyrical passages of the symphony, two of which (on pp.
24-25 and 115-16) are built on the same theme (ex. 8). The
melodic line alone implies fairly unambiguous phrasing,
cadences, and tonality, even if mode is not so clear. But the
accompaniments in these two passages obscure these things.
What seems transparent is subtly clouded and made much
more unstable by more sinister elements, notably dissonances
based on half-steps whose resolutions are delayed, ambiguous,
or lacking altogether. Even the melody alone seems to be
struggling to establish a diatonic mode. Its interfering chromaticism gives yet another feeling to the basic concept of the
interval class of a half-step.[22]

There are many other ways in which something that seems
straightforward turns into something that is not. Several times
new, more regular or stable music begins, only to have ex. 2
creep into it and radically alter its course. Even without ex. 2,
expectations are often set up which are not fulfilled. A simple
but strong accompaniment figure may just dissolve. A climax
may be cut off abruptly. Textures may change unpredictably.
A certain tonality or sound may disappear as suddenly as it
appeared.

Timbre itself is also a prominent agent of tension and
drama. Notable is the use of high ranges in the string section,
string harmonics, and "abnormal" spacing or scoring. The first
and third of these may be observed in ex. 9, a grotesque
cadence on C major. The second of these (harmonics) is responsible for, among much else, an eery, disembodied sound
in a passage near the end of the symphony (on p. 134) which
is marked *allegretto con malinconia*.

If the symphony is so discontinuous in so many ways, what
then holds it together? The answer is: many of the things

which contribute to this discontinuity, but considered from different perspectives. The interaction of the calm and the turbulent, the lyrical and the dramatic, the innocent and the demonic, contributes strongly to the large-scale shape. Not every passage is exclusively on one side or the other: the combination of extremes and the areas "between" them are as important as the tendency to separate them. In general, however, as the symphony develops, homogeneity of texture and sound tends to last longer. The two "worlds" tend towards greater separation but also greater conflict. In one sense continuity increases, but in another sense it decreases.

Of the many pitch-class relationships which contribute to growth and unity in the symphony, those among B^b-B-C-C# are the most important. C gradually emerges as the most prominent of the four. As the influence of B^b decreases, that of C increases, because of its relation to both B and C#. The high C in ex. 3 and in many derivatives of it occasionally remains not only undisplaced in its own range but much extended in time (see p. 14, mm. 3-7; p. 35, m. 2 to p. 36, m. 1; and ex. 5). Two important closings of passages undisturbed by chromatics are also on C (p. 49, mm. 3 to 6; and ex. 9). Early in the symphony, C begins to interfere in C# cadences (see p. 28, m. 5 to p. 29, m. 1; and ex. 10). Later, ex. 10 turns into ex. 11.

From p. 135, m. 6 to the end, the ultimate working out is presented of this and the other tonal clashes. The very end (ex. 12) is cataclysmic: after all the immense struggles of the symphony, C remains — but dies out deep in the bass.

Elsa Thulin wrote a letter to Alfred Cortot about me: "Il a lutté, il a gagné!" Sure I've struggled, but have I won?[23]

Footnotes to Chapter V

1   Allan Pettersson: "Anteckningar", in *Nutida Musik*, vol. 4 no. 4,
    1960-61; p. 19.

2   *Ibid.*; p. 19.

3   Göran Bergendal: "Allan Pettersson? Just det!", in *Röster i Radio*,
    no. 49, Nov. 1968; p. 20.

4   Allan Pettersson: "Intyg", unpublished, dated Stockholm, Sep.
    1975; [p. 1.]

5   Göran Bergendal: "Allan Pettersson? . . ."; p. 20.

6   Frank Hedman: "Allan Pettersson, en ordets man", in Allan Petters-
    son: *Barfotasånger och Andra Dikter* ([Stockholm:] Rabén och
    Sjögren, 1976; p. 7.

7   Several different pairs of dates have been suggested for his tenure
    in the orchestra, but 1940-53 is what the orchestra's own files con-
    tain. From the fall of 1951 to the spring of 1953, he was on leave
    in order to pursue his studies in composition.

8   Allan Pettersson: *Barfotasånger och Andra Dikter*; p. 16.

9   Ironically, this publisher has recently been planning to issue the
    music to the *Barefoot Songs*.

10 Hans Ekheden and Allan Pettersson: "Allan Petterssons första
    stråkkonsert åter efter 20 år", in *Konsertnytt*, vol. 10 no. 15, 5-
    18.V.1975; p. 4.

11 Sigvard Hammar: "Musiken gör livet uthärdligt", in *Dagens Nyheter*,
    Sunday 5 March 1972.

12 Urban Stenström: "Allan Pettersson—komponerande och grub-
    blande son av Söder", in *Nutida Musik*, vol. 1 no. 5, 1958; pp. 6-7.

13 *Ibid.*; p. 8.

14 Funds provided chiefly through S.T.I.M. (Svenska Tonsättares
    Internationella Musikbyrå) have made it possible for copyists to
    produce very good full scores of the works completed after this
    time, although for some performances these have not been available,
    and photocopies of Pettersson's manuscripts have been used.

15 All the records have originated in Sweden, although a few have also
    been released elsewhere.

16 Reidar Storaas: "Musikken er det som tross alt gjør livet verd å leve
    . . .", in *Bergens Tidende*, date unknown but sometime in the week
    preceding 24.X.1974.

17 Allan Pettersson: "Den konstnärliga lögnen", in *Musiklivet*, vol. 28 no. 2, 1955; p. 26.

18 among the symphonies nos. 2 to 11 (no. 1 has been withdrawn, and nos. 12 and 13 are too recent for inclusion in this study).

19 in his notes to the recording of the 6th symphony, CBS 76553.

20 Reidar Storaas: "Musikken er det som . . .".

21 The half-step relations, the main pitch classes, and even the basic gesture may be traced back to ex. 3.

22 The first measure of ex. 8 may be heard as a smoothed-out version of ex. 3.

23 Karl Sjunnesson and Allan Pettersson: [programme notes,] in *Konsertnytt*, vol. 6 no. 1, Sep. 1970; p. 8.

124

OPUS EST

[Allegretto]

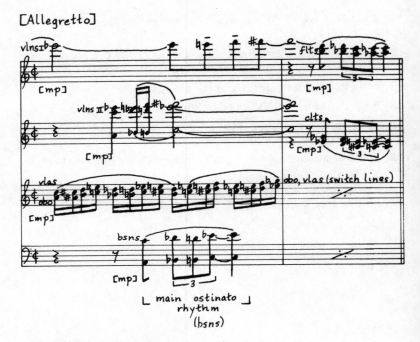

Ex. 1: Symphony No. 9 (p. 105, mm. 1-2)

Ex. 2: Symphony No. 2 (p. 14, mm. 2-4)

Ex. 3: Symphony No. 2 (p. 8, mm. 1-2)

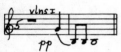

Ex. 4: Symphony No. 2 (p. 5, mm. 2-3)

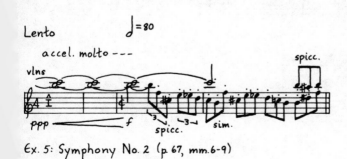

Ex. 5: Symphony No. 2 (p. 67, mm. 6-9)

Ex.6: Symphony No. 2 (p. 120, m.8 to p. 121, m.2; Rom. numerals for top notes only)

Molto tranquillo con sentimento

Ex.7: Symphony No. 2 (p. 45, m.4 to p. 46, m.3)

Ex. 8: Symphony No. 2 (p. 115, mm. 8-14)

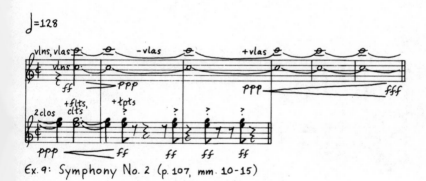

Ex. 9: Symphony No. 2 (p. 107, mm. 10-15)

(From ♩=112 previous measure)
-accel.-------------------

Ex. 10: Symphony No. 2 (p. 42, mm. 4-6)

Rall.------------

Ex. 11: Symphony No. 2 (p. 111, mm. 5-6)

From x to the final ff (tpts, hrns, tbns),
the marking is <u>poco a poco senza sord.</u>

Ex. 12: Symphony No. 2 (p. 138, m. 2 to p. 139, m. 9)

ORCHESTRAL WORKS BY ALLAN PETTERSSON

For an explanation of abbreviations and what is included in this list, see page 19.

CONCERTO FOR STRING ORCHESTRA NO. 1* (1949-50)
1st prf: 6.IV.1952. Tor Mann, Swedish Radio S.O.

SYMPHONY NO. 1 (1950-51?)

SYMPHONY NO. 2* (1952-53)
1st prf: 9.V.1954. Tor Mann, Swedish Radio S.O.

SYMPHONY NO. 3 (1954-55)
1st prf: 21.XI.1956. Tor Mann, Gothenburg Orchestral Society.

CONCERTO FOR STRING ORCHESTRA NO. 2 (1956)
1st prf: 1.XII.1968. Stig Westerberg, Swedish Radio S.O.

CONCERTO FOR STRING ORCHESTRA NO. 3* (1956-57)
1st prf: 14.III.1958. Tor Mann, Swedish Radio S.O.

SYMPHONY NO. 4 (1958-59)
1st prf: 27.I.1961. Sixten Ehrling, Stockholm P.O.

SYMPHONY NO. 5 (1960-62)
1st prf: 8.XI.1963. Stig Westerberg, Swedish Radio S.O.

SYMPHONY NO. 6* (1963-66)
1st prf: 21.I.1968. Stig Westerberg, Swedish Radio S.O.

SYMPHONY NO. 7* (1966-67)
1st prf: 13.X.1968. Antal Doráti, Stockholm P.O.
Pbd: Stockholm. Nordiska Musikförlaget, 1972.

SYMPHONY NO. 8 (1968-69)
1st Prf: 23.II.1972. Antal Doráti, Stockholm P.O.

SYMPHONY NO. 9 (1970)
1st prf: 18.II.1971. Sergiu Comissiona, Gothenburg S.O.

SYMPHONY NO. 10* (1971-72)
1st prf: 16.XII.1973. Antal Doráti, Swedish Radio S.O.

SYMPHONY NO. 11 (1971, 72-73)
1st prf: 24.X.1974. Karsten Andersen, [Bergen] Harmonien Orc.

SYMPHONY NO. 12, *De Döda på Torget* (1973-74)
Note: for chorus and orchestra.

ALLAN PETTERSSON   131

SYMPHONIC MOVEMENT (1973)
1st prf: 24.XII.1976. Stig Westerberg, Swedish Radio S.O.

VOX HUMANA* (1974)
1st prf: 19.III.1976. Stig Westerberg, cdr.; Swedish Radio
              S.O.; Swedish Radio Chorus; Marianne Mellnäs, sopra-
              no; Margot Rödin, alto; Sven-Erik Alexandersson,
              tenor; Erland Hagegård, baritone.
Note: orchestra is strings only.

SYMPHONY NO. 13 (1976)

OTHER WORKS

six songs (1935); 24 Barefoot Songs (1943-45); concerto for violin and
string quartet (1949); seven sonatas for two violins (1951); concerto for
violin and orchestra (1977).

DISCOGRAPHY OF ORCHESTRAL WORKS IN THE MAIN LIST

CONCERTO FOR STRING ORCHESTRA NO. 1. Stig Westerberg,
Swedish Radio S.O. Caprice CAP 1110 (with Lidholm: Nausicaa
Ensam).

SYMPHONY NO. 2. Stig Westerberg, Swedish Radio S.O. a) Decca SXL
6265. b) Swedish Society Discofil SLT 33219.

CONCERTO FOR STRING ORCHESTRA NO. 3: second movement
only, Mesto. Stig Westerberg, Swedish Radio S.O. a) Swedish
Society Discofil LT 33158 (mono) and SLT 33158 (both with
Eklund: Music for Orchestra). b) Swedish Society Discofil SLT
33203 (with Sibelius: The Tempest).

SYMPHONY NO. 6. Okko Kamu, Norrköping S.O. CBS 76553.

SYMPHONY NO. 7. Antal Doráti, Stockholm P.O. a) Expo Norr RIKS
LP 15. b) Caprice CAP 1015. c) Decca SXL 6538. d) London
(U.S.A.) CS 6740. e) Swedish Society Discofil SLT 33194.

SYMPHONY NO. 10. Antal Doráti, Swedish Radio S.O. EMI 4E 061-
35142 (with Blomdahl: Symphony No. 2).

VOX HUMANA. Stig Westerberg, cdr.; Swedish Radio S.O.; Swedish
Radio Chorus; Marianne Mellnäs, soprano; Margot Rödin, alto;
Sven-Erik Alexandersson, tenor; Erland Hagegård, baritone. BIS
LP-55.

ORCHESTRAL AUTOGRAPH MANUSCRIPTS

Most of these are at S.T.I.M.'s Information Centre for Swedish Music, Stockholm.

SELECTED WRITINGS BY ALLAN PETTERSSON

"Att fiska toner", in *Röster i Radio*, early Apr. 1952.

"Dissonance—douleur", in *Musique Contemporaine—Revue Internationale*, nos. 4-6, 1952; pp. 235-36.

"Den konstnärliga lögnen", in *Musiklivet*, vol. 28 no. 2, 1955; pp. 26-27.

"Allan Pettersson: Konsert nr 3 för stråkorkester", in *Nutida Musik*, vol. 1 no. 5, 1958; pp. 14-16.

"Anteckningar", in *Nutida Musik*, vol. 4 no. 4, 1960-61; p. 19.

[letter to Leif Aare,] in Leif Aare: "Identifikation med det oansenliga", in *Nutida Musik*, vol. 12 no. 2, 1968-69; pp. 55-56.

[with Hans Ekheden] "Allan Petterssons första stråkkonsert åter efter 20 år", in *Konsertnytt*, vol. 10 no. 15, 5-18.V.1975; pp. 4-6.

SELECTED WRITINGS BY OTHERS ABOUT PETTERSSON

Urban Stenström: "Allan Pettersson—komponerande och grubblande son av Söder", in *Nutida Musik*, vol. 1 no. 5, 1958; pp. 6-11.

Göran Fant: "Den sista symfonikern", in *Nutida Musik*, vol. 7 no. 2, 1963-64; pp. 11-13.

Göran Bergendal: "Allan Pettersson? Just det!", in *Röster i Radio*, no. 49, Nov. 1968; pp. 18-20.

Göran Bergendal: "Allan Pettersson", in his *33 Svenska Komponister* (Stockholm: Lindblad, 1972); pp. 207-13.

Rolf Davidson: "Om Allan Petterssons sextiotalssymfonier", in *Nutida Musik*, vol. 17 no. 2, 1973-74; pp. 30-36.

Leif Aare: "Människans röst i det onda samhället", in *Nutida Musik*, vol. 19 no. 3, 1975-76; pp. 32-34.

*Fartein Valen, probably in the late 1920's
or early 1930's*

VI   Fartein Valen and his Four Orchestral Works Opus 17 and Opus 18

He is glad to be at peace without disturbances of any kind; the only thing he is interested in is that what he creates shall be preserved for the future. He has no ambition, is free within.[1]

The two most important sources of inspiration for Fartein Valen's music were probably Christianity and nature. This is strongly suggested by the texts he set in his vocal and choral works and the titles of his nine short orchestral works. It is documented by his discussions with his friends of ideas behind these and other compositions.

Lasting experiences of religion and nature came when he was very young. Valen was born in Stavanger, Norway on 25 August 1887; he spent several of his early years on Madagascar, where his parents were devoted missionaries.[2] Even late in life, Valen remembered many aspects of his life there, particularly the people, the plants, and the animals. Upon the Valens' return to Stavanger in the mid-1890's, his parents took charge of a home for children of missionaries. A great deal of the religious life of the community centred around them.

Valen began school in Stavanger, and his interest in music, already evident on Madagascar, increased rapidly. His most important early teacher in music was the pianist Jeanette Mohr, whose sons Otto (later a geneticist) and Hugo (later a painter) became close friends of his.[3] Before he was twelve, Valen was writing large numbers of short compositions. By the time he graduated from the gymnasium in 1906, he had decided to pursue a musical career, but his father had other ideas. The resulting compromise was that Valen went to Oslo

[1]   See footnotes p. 149

in 1906 to study languages at the university but also music theory with Catharinus Elling. After his father died, Valen went in 1907 to the music conservatory in Oslo, where in 1909 he graduated with distinction in organ and theory.

That year Valen had a composition published for the first time: a *Legend* for piano written in 1907. Also in 1909 he applied to the Berlin *Hochschule für Musik* and was admitted by its director Max Bruch after Bruch had examined a few of Valen's compositions: Valen had arrived in Berlin too late for the formal entrance examinations. Valen spent 1909 to 1911 there studying composition, piano, singing, counterpoint, and music history. But on the whole he was dissatisfied with the school's teaching of composition through purely technical analysis of works from the past. In reference to this, Valen once said, "I thought I had come to a temple of art, but it was only a seminary for musicians."[4]

Nonetheless, the opportunities for attending musical performances of all kinds, especially orchestral, were so great in Berlin that Valen stayed there and taught privately until 1916. His own studies concentrated on music from the renaissance onwards. As his already considerable love for Bach deepened, he began during this time to write as exercises six fugues on each of the 48 fugue subjects from *Das Wohltemperierte Klavier*.

In his original compositions, he was moving away from chromatic tonality towards a contrapuntal atonality whose pitch relations were not unlike those found in some of Schoenberg's preserial atonal music. In most other ways, his music was very un-Schoenbergian, notably in its treatment of thematicism, rhythm, and emotional contrasts. Valen was, however, much impressed by Schoenberg's music that he heard and studied in Berlin.[5] He retained a life-long admiration for it when most of musical Norway was ignorant of it and (later) could not tolerate it.

Valen spent the period 1916 to 1932 back in Norway — the first eight years mostly at his parents' home near Valevåg on the west coast, the second eight years mostly in Oslo. In 1917, convinced that he had to work out for himself new principles of composition based on dissonance rather than consonance, he began a series of short exercises which he kept producing for at least 25 years and which is said to contain about 27000 items. He was also in no hurry to complete compositions: he struggled with his opus 4 and opus 5 for many years before he was satisfied with them. The latter, a piano trio, he worked on possibly for eleven years, producing over 1200 pages of sketches for it.

In 1917 Valen also had his first public success, through Dagny Knutsen's Oslo performance of his first piano sonata, op. 2. In his Valen biography, Olav Gurvin implies that around this time, the handsome young composer was more or less pursued by various young women.[6] He never married, however, possibly because of his devotion to his religion and his music. Another reason may have been his health. Throughout his life he was very rarely in excellent health; aftereffects of malaria (which he had caught on Madagascar) and various nervous and respiratory disorders often made work very difficult for him. His general frailty may have precluded marriage in his mind. It certainly accounted in part for his shy and retiring character, his avoidance of publicity, and his uncomfortable feeling in the company of any but his family and his closest friends. In 1922 during a stay at a *pensione* in Rome, the owner's daughter, a violinist, found out that Valen was the composer of a violin sonata she had recently played. Valen was pleased by the coincidence. He was also pleased that it was discovered on the *last* day of his stay at the *pensione*, because he would otherwise have had much less peace and quiet there to continue his work.[7]

After his mother's death in 1923, Valen moved to Oslo. He never liked Oslo but could not avoid it, as it was, for better or worse, Norway's cultural centre. Five years earlier he had written:

> Only a little while ago Beethoven was dull — like all "German music". Chaykovskiy was the great master. Then came Romain Rolland's Beethoven biography, and suddenly all of Snobiania[8] turned right around: Beethoven suddenly became first-rate . . . I go only reluctantly to Kristiania; I have quite honestly had enough of the whole attitude in [its] music circles, this defaming of all good music, and all the superficiality and pomposity. For me Kr[istiania] represents the epitomy of philistinism and lack of culture and taste in regard to music.[9]

Oslo was where Valen had to make his name and where solid employment in music could be found. He took on private pupils in piano, theory, and composition. Most of his own works from this time were songs, but he also wrote two string quartets. In 1925 he was awarded a small government grant for two years, after which he was put in charge of the newly established Norwegian Music Collection in the University of Oslo library. In the early 1930's his works were played and published with some frequency, although critical opinion was sharply divided. In 1931 and 1932 Valen received further awards which enabled him to travel to Mallorca, where he spent seven months in 1932-33. There he worked on several orchestral compositions which will be discussed shortly. His production in the years 1930 to 1934 was in fact dominated by short works for orchestra; during that time he completed eight of them. In the same period the conductor Olav Kielland helped him greatly by conducting four of them in Oslo.

From 1933 to 1938 Valen was mostly in Oslo, teaching and composing as before. The publisher Norsk Musikforlag, which had issued several of his works, became less interested in him and published nothing of his after 1937. This was a severe loss to him, but it was more than made up for financially by the award of a Civil List grant for life in 1935. This permitted him eventually to give up teaching. In 1938 he moved back to Valevåg, where he could live undisturbed in his native region, surrounded by the natural setting he loved.

The 1930's were probably the most difficult years for him, despite the fact that his works were being heard more than before. Much of Norwegian musical life was strongly nationalistic. As Norway had been a completely independent country only since 1905, a lot of energy was spent on building a distinctive Norwegian culture in every domain in the two decades following the first world war. Valen did not fit into this scheme at all. His music was not based on recognizably Norwegian elements, musical or otherwise. His more internationally oriented atonal polyphony thus gained him opponents in large measure because of the Norwegian political situation.

Both biographies of Valen mention that he was often worried that others were working against him. Adverse criticism of his music, which was common, often upset him a great deal, even later in his career when he knew there was enough favourable criticism to balance it. When his name was first put forward for the Civil List grant and he did not win it (1934), he was sure his opponents had supported the winner mainly to put him down. Thus the award to Valen the following year seemed as much a political victory as a financial relief. After the second world war, however, the grant stopped suddenly. Valen "was afraid it was evil tongues that had been at work, and dreaded to complain."[10] But after a few months he had to complain, and the grant was continued.

Although he often felt wronged, he rarely had the strength or desire to advance his causes. Many performances and honours would not have come to him if it were not for his friends' work. When it came to matters he alone could deal with, he sometimes did nothing, reasoning that his efforts would create more problems than solutions. Gurvin tells a story[11] of Valen declining to correct a persistent performance error at a rehearsal of one of his orchestral works, presumably in the mid- to late 1940's. Valen preferred hoping for a better performance in the future to creating embarrassment and irritation by pointing out the error. He was also glad to note that the musicians were quite interested in his music and no longer played it as they had in the 1930's, with obvious dislike for it.

On other occasions, musicians asked for changes in certain places in certain works. To this, however, Valen said no, believing that some day better instruments or better performers would produce what he imagined.

This faith in himself and the future enabled him to continue his work, especially during the second world war and the German occupation of Norway. At this time there was not enough fuel for lamps (Valevåg first got electricity a few years after the war), especially during the long winters. Despite this and his decreasing physical strength, during the war he completed three large works and most of a fourth: a violin concerto, a piano sonata, and his second and third symphonies.

After the war his fame increased. In 1947, on his 60th birthday, the Norwegian press gave him great acclaim. That year and the next, two works were played at I.S.C.M. festivals, one in Copenhagen (1947), the other in Amsterdam (1948).

In 1947, under the instigation of Philip Krømer of Harald
Lyche and Company, Lyche gave Valen a publishing contract
which guaranteed him further steady income. In the 30 years
since then, Lyche has published, in addition to other Valen
compositions and Gurvin's biography of him, all but two of
the 13 purely orchestral works extant which were not published earlier by Norsk Musikforlag.

Another significant event in 1947 was the premiere of the
violin concerto; a few years later it was recorded. A film was
made of its performance and shown in the 1950's in several
countries including England. The pianist Aleksandr Helmann,
having attended the concerto's premiere, became very interested in Valen's music and asked him to write him a piano
concerto. That concerto became Valen's last completed composition.[12] Helmann also helped start a Fartein Valen Society,
whose first publication, in 1952, was the violin concerto. The
society still exists.[13]

In his last five years, Valen's strength gradually declined.
He found it difficult to complete laborious tasks, such as ac-
knowledging the many letters and gifts he received for his 60th
birthday, and writing out full scores of compositions he considered already essentially complete in short score. He left
three works in varying stages of completeness: a fifth symphony, a *Kyrie* movement to a mass, and music to accompany
a reading of H.C. Andersen's *The Story of a Mother*. He died
on 14 December 1952.

The story of what Valen did or did not complete does not
end here, however. When Valen died, all his music manuscripts
and many letters he wrote were placed in the University of
Oslo library but were not made available to the public. In
1953-54 the librarian Helge Kragemoe catalogued the material
and sealed most of it with the following restriction:

Restriction on Fartein Valen's manuscripts.

   Exercises, preliminary studies, sketches, and letters are en-
trusted to the U[niversity] L[ibrary] with the restriction that
they shall not be used without Dr. O[lav] Gurvin's permission before 1. Jan. 1978. Should he pass away before then, the oldest,
permanent univ[ersity] teacher in musicology shall have the right
of decision. Access shall also be given only after consultation with
Valen's nearest, oldest relative.

9. Sept. 1953.
H[elge] Kr[agemoe]

In late 1976 this was replaced by a more specific and much less ambiguous restriction. Certain manuscripts (within the library numbers mus. mss. 4501-65, the collection of letters 277, the mss. 8⁰ 2544 and 2813, the mss. 4⁰ 2276), which include the Valen material covered by the earlier restriction, can now not be used before 14 December 2002 without permission from "1) the professor of musicology at the University of Oslo who has the longest seniority, and 2) the representative for Fartein Valen's family who at any time is administring the rights to his works".[14] Other Valen items, chiefly fair copies of full scores and some drafts for these, can be seen but not copied without the same two persons' permission. The new restriction concludes with the statement "Copyright for all Valen's music manuscripts belongs to Harald Lyche and Co. Music Publisher".[15]

In his Valen biography, Gurvin says that Valen burned many early manuscripts and might have burned more, to prevent their misuse by those who would harm him. He also says that Valen eventually suggested keeping his remaining exercises, sketches, and letters generally inaccessible for 25 or 50 years after his death and that Valen gave him authority to take care of the matter.

Bjarne Kortsen, Valen's other biographer, who has published many other books about him, disputes the essence of this. He says that the restrictions placed on the use of Valen's material are not in accord with Valen's wishes as they were expressed to him not long before Valen died.

Kortsen came to have many disputes with Gurvin and later with several others involved with Valen's music. One of the most interesting centres around Valen's piano concerto. Kortsen discovered important discrepancies between the published version and what he was certain was Valen's final fair copy of the work. He wrote about the matter to the publisher (Lyche) and to Valen's relative in charge of the composer's legacy. Getting no satisfaction after a period of time, he turned to government officials, charged that in their publication of the concerto Lyche had violated a law concerning works of art, and asked that Lyche be required legally to mention in the published score where, why, and by whom certain editorial decisions had been made.

The only easily accessible report of what then took place is

Kortsen's own,[16] which can scarcely be considered wholly representative of everyone's opinions. However, the report seems to carry enough direct quotation to give a good idea of the official results of the enquiry. A Board of Experts for Works of Art, drawn up by the Royal Ministry of Church and Education Affairs, decided that there were indeed inconsistencies in the editing of the concerto. Kortsen had been right about some points, wrong about some, and had not mentioned others. The board also decided that Lyche and Co. should have mentioned the editorial practice but could not be forced to do so, and that Lyche had not violated the law Kortsen had mentioned.

The board's report on specific editorial problems in the concerto took into account Valen's three autograph manuscript copies of it (one draft and two full scores). One of the recurring questions was whether Valen made errors or changed things deliberately in writing out the second orchestral score from the first. The question is difficult. Valen was probably unwell when he wrote some parts of the scores, and in any case there is no precedent of his writing out two full scores of an orchestral work. Unfortunately, the Board of Experts seems not to have gained the necessary familiarity with Valen's late style, both musical and chirographical, from more than the one composition. This is the main drawback in the attempt to resolve the dispute.

Whether most of Valen's manuscript material should be subject to restricted use until the end of the year 2002 remains a central question, even if it is not answerable. Who is permitted to study and write about what part of the legacy can be answered only by individuals applying for the necessary permissions. Yet certain fundamental subjects can not be properly treated without access to a great many, perhaps all of the manuscripts, e.g. the development of Valen's working methods or his relationship to Schoenberg's music and ideas. Furthermore, Gurvin's and Kortsen's biographies contain substantial errors, omissions, and ambiguities in matters such as dating — errors, etc. which are obvious without recourse to the restricted materials. Gurvin may have made use of the materials, but both books require checking with the original sources to verify a great deal — "simple facts" such as dates, more complex interpretations of data, and everything in between. Irrespective of obvious errors, research should not rely on secondary sources when primary sources are available. The study which says that Gurvin and Kortsen "both knew him [Valen] personally, as a friend, and there is no reason to doubt the authenticity of what they have to tell us"[17] makes a fundamental and fatal error comparable to believing that everything said in a court of law is 100% correct merely because it is said under oath. In any case, Valen's own wishes on the disposition of his manuscripts remain unclear. But the current restrictions on them must be understood by all potential users of them.

There is more confusion in the Valen literature over his four short orchestral works published under op. 17 and op. 18 than over any others. Gurvin says in one place (his biography, p. 93) that all four were completed in 1932, but in another (his biography, p. 199) he notes that one or two have final dates in 1933. Some of his dates disagree with what is on Valen's manuscripts themselves and what is in Kragemoe's catalogue of the restricted materials. Kortsen makes some of the same mistakes in his biography. With reference to most of Valen's works, neither author consistently distinguishes between a sketch and a (generally three-stave) short score. In Kragemoe's catalogue, the latter is sometimes mislabelled a piano score.

The four works in question are as follows:

> *Sonetto di Michelangelo*, op. 17 no. 1
> *Cantico di Ringraziamento*, op. 17 no. 2
> *Nenia*, op. 18 no. 1
> *An die Hoffnung*, op. 18 no. 2

They have many features in common and also resemble the other five short, one-movement orchestral works. Like the others, these four may be considered studies for the later multi-movement symphonies. But they stand on their own as predominantly lyrical epigrams, with a power which is partly attributable to their very brevity and simplicity of means.

All four works use Valen's own concepts of atonal polyphony. Each is hyperthematic in that nearly every note is part of one of the melodic shapes clearly announced at the beginning of the work. Formally, each consists of waves of tension and relaxation which are built out of numerous contrapuntal combinations of these shapes. Tension in these works is a function chiefly of dynamics, range of sonorities, and texture. Tempos rarely change; small-scale rhythms and orchestration as such are quite straightforward. Valen's orchestration has in fact been criticized as unadventurous, but it is so only "on paper". Its simplicity is largely responsible for the elegance and clarity of these works and the sense of vast "aural space" which they impart.

Gurvin and Kortsen both identify the sonnet that lay behind *Sonetto di Michelangelo*.[18] Neither mentions that the published score prints only the first eight lines of it; both authors reprint these lines as if they were the whole sonnet. Valen may have wanted the last six lines omitted, but the poem's meaning is radically altered by their omission.

Gurvin and Kortsen also discuss the four works as if they were written in the order indicated by their opus numbers. They do not note that at least two of them may not always have carried the opus numbers they were published with. Ex. 1 contains the dating evidence. "(G)" signifies material obtained solely from Gurvin's biography. The sources for ex.1 are that book, Kragemoe's catalogue, and materials which were not restricted (by the special clauses mentioned earlier) in early to mid-June 1976.

Gurvin's dates may not be reliable. But with or without them, one can see that the correct ordering might be *Sonetto-Nenia-Cantico-An die Hoffnung*. It is true that Valen may have worked on most of the orchestral score of *Nenia* after most of the orchestral score of *Cantico*. But he may also have considered their *short* scores complete in all essentials. Gurvin quotes two letters from him concerning *Cantico* which support this idea.[19]

Further complications are provided by the opus numbers themselves. The programme note from the first performance of *Cantico* groups *Sonetto-Nenia-Cantico* in that order as op. 17 (nos. 1, 2, and 3 respectively) and *An die Hoffnung* and *Epithalamion* as op. 18 (nos. 1 and 2 respectively). Some but not all reviews of the first performances of both *Sonetto* and *Cantico* mention or imply a triptych of which *Cantico* is the *last* member.[20]

The accessible autograph music manuscripts are also part of the problem. *Epithalamion* is not put into op. 18. The designation "op. 17 no. 2" on the title page of *Cantico* has the 2 written over something else, probably a 3. The first title page of *Nenia* reads "op. 18 no. 1", but the second title page and the first page of the music have what may be "op. 17 no. 2" with the 2 written over a 1 — although it is possible that the 1 was written over the 2. All that can be firmly concluded from this and similar evidence is that Valen changed his mind one or more times on the numbering. He eventually settled on the numbers as they appear in the printed scores and in the list of works at the end of this chapter: his own list from the mid-1940's has them that way. But he may indeed at one time have put three works into op. 17 or put *Nenia* before *Cantico*.

The matter of the dating, numbering, and ordering of these four orchestral works is more than an irrelevant curiosity. At the least, the confusion suggests that a look at the music might *not* reveal any musical reasons why one grouping should be preferred over another. What sharp differences could be expected in four works that were written one after another in less than a year?

As has been noted, in general style the four works reveal few differences. But in specific details there are several differences which show how much closer to *Sonetto Nenia* is than *Cantico* is. Exs. 2 to 4 contain the basic thematic-motivic material of these three works. Each example is divided into three parts. The first parts (A, D, and G) emphasize adjacent melodic interval classes of seconds and thirds; the second parts (B, E, and H) emphasize fourths — but they are perfect fourths in parts B and E and augmented fourths in part H (from *Cantico*). In the third parts of *Sonetto* and *Nenia* (parts C and F), seconds and thirds are re-emphasized; in *Cantico* (part I) they are mixed with equally prominent fourths. The tripartite division in each example is brought about by rhythmic, registral, and/or orchestration changes, but these changes are much greater in *Sonetto* and *Nenia*. Ex. 4 is more continuous; it is the subject of the five-voice fugue which constitutes *Cantico*.

Further points suggest that *Cantico* is the odd one out in this group of three. *Sonetto* and *Nenia* are more subtle in delineating large-scale formal sectioning than *Cantico*. Their overall dynamic design might be indicated as <>, whereas *Cantico*'s would be <. And although the large-scale formal importance of triplets in *Sonetto* and *Nenia* is slight, it is much greater in *Cantico*: the third of *Cantico*'s four sections begins with a sudden change to triplet presentation of the fugue theme (ex. 5).

In smaller-scale matters, sequence and exact pitch repetition are more important, phrases are longer, and the analogies to tonal functions are more pronounced in *Cantico* than in the other two. The endings of *Sonetto* and *Nenia* are tonally indeterminate (see exs. 6 and 7). *Cantico* ends in a definite key of G, although it is defined by "dissonant polyphony", or more accurately, by voice leading based on discords with emphasis on equal-temperament approximations of higher overtones. Ex. 8 shows the essential harmonic and contrapuntal plan of *Cantico*'s last five measures. One possible outer-voice reduction of this is ex. 9. The concordant G-D perfect fifth is a dissonance which resolves to the more discordant D^b-D consonance.

In still simpler matters, *Cantico* uses a larger orchestra, has more independent parts (up to five), and is noticeably longer than the other two works. The variety of timbral combinations and the complexity of the counterpoint and rhythms are also greater in *Cantico*.

Arguments could be made that in a few ways *Nenia* and *Cantico* are similar while *Sonetto* is different. But on grounds of total musical similarity, the other theoretical pairing (of *Sonetto* and *Cantico*) is by far the least likely. Considering Valen's development as a composer from the perspective of his entire production, it is, although not impossible, very unlikely that he wrote one work (*Sonetto*) followed by a very different one (*Cantico*) followed by a third one (*Nenia*) which returns in *so many* ways to characteristics of the first.

The question of why these three works might have once been considered a unit and *An die Hoffnung* a separate work with a separate opus number is not as easy to answer. The simplest explanation for this is that the first three all have an Italian or at least Mediterranean source of inspiration and have Italian titles.

In some ways *An die Hoffnung* resembles *Sonetto* and *Nenia*: it uses a similar orchestra, its dynamic shape is <>, its larger formal divisions are not pronounced, and triplets do not help to mark them. But like *Cantico*, it makes considerable use of immediate repetition of a melodic gesture in the same voice, it contains long passages building to and relaxing from climaxes, and it has distinct tonal references, ending also in G.

Quite different from anything in these other three orchestral works is *An die Hoffnung*'s definitely non-tripartite introduction of as many as seven distinct melodic segments. These are shown in ex. 10. Their comparatively narrow interval span (none exceeds a tenth) and the frequent repetition in *An die Hoffnung* of segment no. 5 (and to a lesser extent no. 1) help give the work a quiet, meditative character. Could the repetitions relate to the repetitive language and structure of the often-mentioned impetus behind *An die Hoffnung*, namely John Keats's *To Hope*? Segments nos. 1, 5, and 6 are combined and repeated a great deal in the final eight measures in a key of G that is even clearer than the one at the end of *Cantico*. At the end of *An die Hoffnung* (see ex. 11), the use of these segments implies a very stable complete tonic 13th chord: all seven tones are left "hanging".

The harp is silent until the last six measures. The score permits substitution there of celesta or piano. Kortsen concludes that "the timbre of the harp is actually not very much needed here".[21] But the harp seems especially appropriate in view of the repeated images related to heaven at the end of all eight stanzas of Keats's poem. Notwithstanding the celestial references, the celesta would be too thin and bright. The piano would be a little too heavy and would lack the celestial connotation.

The higher degree of repetition and the more obvious tonality in *An die Hoffnung* may be considered further explorations of directions found in the previous three orchestral works, taken in the order *Sonetto-Nenia-Cantico*.[22] Other tendencies become more pronounced in both *Cantico* and *An die Hoffnung*. For example, there is a decrease in the use of climactic repetition of motives at the same pitch level and leading to longer held notes. And in *An die Hoffnung* there is no equivalent to the figure comprising the last four notes in ex. 2, which are used only to end a phrase. In both *Cantico* and *An die Hoffnung*, nonfinal dissolutions become less complete and predictable, and the climaxes themselves become longer.

None of these things implies higher or lower quality of composition as the series of four works unfolds, but they do point towards more extended scope in orchestral movements, which Valen later achieved more fully in the symphonies.

To return to the initial questions concerning these four works: the confusion over dating and opus numbers leads to necessary examinations of the music itself for possible clues to these matters. These examinations reveal subtle differences in the four works, differences which are possibly more interesting than the original problems. In any case, most indications, both internal and external, suggest that *Nenia* predates *Cantico*. Valen may have settled on the opus numbers he did for many reasons — he may even have liked the parallel phrasing of the two titles in op. 17 and the balance of *nenia* against *Hoffnung* in op. 18. Perhaps his sketches and letters will reveal more information on these and related matters.

Footnotes to Chapter VI

1 Fartein Valen and Else Christie Kielland: "Selvbiografiske data", in *Nordisk Musikkultur*, vol. 6 no. 4, Dec. 1969; p. 166. Valen dictated this article to Kielland, referring to himself throughout in the third person.

2 He had gone to Madagascar with his parents in 1889.

3 Much later, both brothers assisted Valen greatly in many ways when he encountered difficulties with his composing career.

4 Olav Gurvin: *Fartein Valen—En Banebryter i Nyere Norsk Musikk* (Drammen: Harald Lyche, 1962); p. 44.

5 In an important letter to his sister Magnhild of 19.XI.1913, Valen told how fascinated he was by a Schoenberg quartet he had heard. Unfortunately he did not specify the quartet or even the year in which he heard it. One of Valen's biographers (Olav Gurvin) says it was Schoenberg's Quartet No. 1, the other (Bjarne Kortsen) says it was no. 2.

6 Olav Gurvin: *Fartein Valen* . . . ; p. 65.

7 *Ibid.*; p. 73.

8 As can be noted from the last sentence of this whole quotation, Oslo was still called Kristiania at this time.

9 Olav Gurvin: *Fartein Valen* . . . ; p. 68.

10 *Ibid.*; p. 140.

11 *Ibid.*; p. 164.

12 Helmann became ill and died before being able to play the concerto. Valen never heard it either, as its first performance took place a month after his own death.

13 Its current address is Postboks 1817, Vika, Oslo 1, Norway.

14 Magne Valen-Sendstad: letter to Paul Rapoport dated Stavanger, 2.IX.1976.

15 Øystein Gaukstad: letter to Paul Rapoport dated Oslo, 18.XI.1976.

16 Bjarne Kortsen: *Utgivelsen av Fartein Valens Klaverkonsert Op. 44* (Bergen: Bjarne Kortsen, 1971).

17. Florence Leah Windebank: *The Music of Fartein Valen. 1887-1952* (unpublished thesis, London, 1973); p. 12.

18. It begins: Non so se s'è la desiata luce
del suo primo fattor, che l'alma sente

19 Olav Gurvin: *Fartein Valen* . . . ; pp. 99-100.

20   See Bjarne Kortsen: *Gjennom Kamp til Seier—Førstefremføringer av Fartein Valens Musikk i Norsk Presse gjennom Ca. 40 År* (Oslo: Bjarne Kortsen, 1963); pp. 69-86.

21   Bjarne Kortsen: *Fartein Valen: Life and Music* Volume 2 (Oslo: Johan Grundt Tanum, 1965); p. 208.

22   It is interesting that Valen's next work, *Epithalamion*, op. 19, is the most repetitive and tonal of any of his nine short orchestral works.

	Sonetto di Michelangelo	Cantico di Ringraziamento	Nenia	An die Hoffnung
preparatory work	11.III.1932 to 6.VII.1932 (??) (G)	6.VIII.1932 to 12.IX.1932 (G)	20.VII.1932 to 4.VIII.1932 (G)	missing?
short score	missing?	8.VIII.1932 to 28.XII.1932	27.VII.1932 to 4.VIII.1932	26.I.1933 to 17.II.1933
full orchestral score	17.VI.1932 to ? [no date]	? [no date] to 17.I.1933	? [no date] to 23.I.1933	no dates

Ex.1: Four orchestral works opus 17 and opus 18 (dates of composition)

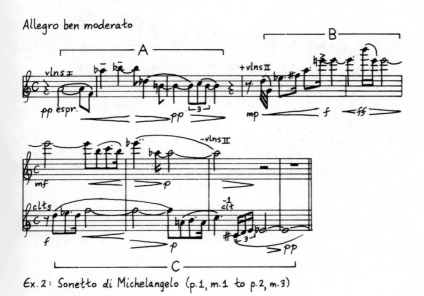

Ex.2: Sonetto di Michelangelo (p.1, m.1 to p.2, m.3)

Moderato

Ex. 3: Nenia (p. 3, m. 1 to p. 4, m. 1; p. 4, mm. 5-7)

Allegro moderato

Ex. 4: Cantico di Ringraziamento (p. 3, m. 1 to p. 4, m. 2)

Allegro moderato

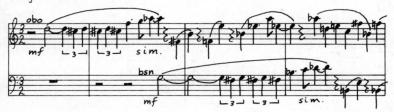

Ex. 5: Cantico di Ringraziamento (p. 14, m. 2 to p. 15, m. 1)

Allegro ben moderato

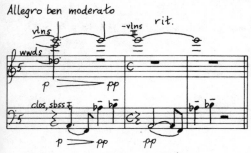

Ex. 6: Sonetto di Michelangelo (p. 15, mm. 3-5)

Moderato

Ex. 7: Nenia (p. 12, mm. 6-9)

Ex. 8: Cantico di Ringraziamento (reduction of p. 25, m. 1 to p. 26, m. 3)

Ex. 9: Cantico di Ringraziamento (outer-voice reduction of p. 25, m. 1 to
p. 26, m. 3)

Moderato, fliessend

Ex. 10: An die Hoffnung (melodic segments from p.3, m.0 to p.4, m.6)

[Tranquillo]

Ex. 11: An die Hoffnung (p.15, mm. 7-9)

ORCHESTRAL WORKS BY FARTEIN VALEN (from 1907 onwards)

For an explanation of abbreviations and what is included in this list, see page 19.

PASTORALE, op. 11* (1929-30)
1st prf: 9.III.1931. Olav Kielland, [Oslo] Philharmonic Society Orc.
Pbd: Oslo. Norsk Musikforlag, 1933.

SONETTO DI MICHELANGELO, op. 17 no. 1* (1932)
1st prf: 15.I.1934. Olav Kielland, [Oslo] Philharmonic Society Orc.
Pbd: Oslo. Norsk Musikforlag, 1936.

NENIA, op. 18 no. 1* (1932-33)
1st prf: 2.V.1952. Odd Grüner-Hegge, [Oslo] Philharmonic Society Orc.
Pbd: Drammen. Harald Lyche, 1960 (but copyright 1954).

CANTICO DI RINGRAZIAMENTO, op. 17 no. 2* (1932-33)
1st prf: 2.X.1933. Olav Kielland, [Oslo] Philharmonic Society Orc.
Pbd: Drammen. Harald Lyche, 1960 (but copyright 1959).

AN DIE HOFFNUNG, op. 18 no. 2* (1932-33)
1st prf: 21.VI.1959. Sverre Bruland, [Oslo] Philharmonic Society Orc.
Pbd: Oslo. Norsk Musikforlag, 1937.

EPITHALAMION, op. 19* (1933)
1st prf: 6.III.1958. Øivin Fjeldstad, [Oslo] Philharmonic Society Orc.
Pbd: Drammen. Harald Lyche, 1972 (but copyright 1958).

LE CIMETIÈRE MARIN, op. 20* (1933-34)
1st prf: 16.XI.1934. Olav Kielland, [Oslo] Philharmonic Society Orc.
Pbd: Drammen. Harald Lyche, 1951.

LA ISLA DE LAS CALMAS, op. 21* (1934)
1st prf: 6.III.1949. Odd Grüner-Hegge, [Oslo] Philharmonic Society Orc.
Pbd: Drammen. Harald Lyche, 1949 (but copyright 1948).

SYMPHONY NO. 1, op. 30 (1937-39)
1st prf: 2.II.1956. Carl Garaguly, [Bergen] Harmonien Orc.

ODE TIL ENSOMHETEN, op. 35* (1939)
1st prf: 24.IV.1955. Carl Garaguly, [Bergen] Harmonien Orc.
Pbd: Drammen. Harald Lyche, 1965 (but copyright 1955).

SYMPHONY NO. 2, op. 40 (1941-44)
1st prf: 28.III.1957. Odd Grüner-Hegge, [Oslo] Philharmonic
              Society Orc.
Pbd: Drammen. Harald Lyche, 1962 (but copyright 1956).

SYMPHONY NO. 3, op. 41 (1944-46)
1st prf: 13.IV.1951. Øivin Fjeldstad, [Oslo] Philharmonic
              Society Orc.
Pbd: Drammen. Harald Lyche, 1954 (but copyright 1949).

SYMPHONY NO. 4, op. 43 (1947-49)
1st prf: 16.X.1956. Sten Åke Axelson, Malmö S.O.

OTHER WORKS (from 1907 onwards)

incomplete symphony (no. 5, 1951-52); possibly incomplete incidental
music to H.C. Andersen's *The Story of a Mother* (1952); concertos for
violin and orchestra (1940), for piano and orchestra (1949-51); two
string quartets (1928-29, 1930-31); piano trio (1913-24); sonata for
violin and piano (1913-18); nine works for piano, two for organ (both
organ works 1939); several motets and songs unaccompanied, with
piano, and with orchestra.

DISCOGRAPHY OF ORCHESTRAL WORKS IN THE MAIN LIST

PASTORALE@. Miltiades Caridis, [Oslo] Philharmonic Society Orc.
Philips 6754 001 is the number of a two-record set which also contains Valen's *Sonetto di Michelangelo*@, *Nenia*@, *Cantico di Ringraziamento, An die Hoffnung, Le Cimetière Marin*@, *La Isla de las
Calmas, Ode til Ensomheten*, and his songs *Ave Maria*@, *Zwei
Chinesische Gedichte*@, *Darest Thou Now O Soul*, and *Die Dunkle
Nacht der Seele*. The conductor and orchestra in all the works are
the same; the soprano in the songs is Dorothy Dorow. The record
number for the works marked @ above is 6507 016, for the others
6507 017.

SONETTO DI MICHELANGELO. Øivin Fjeldstad, [Oslo] Philharmonic
Society Orc. a) Musica KN 7101 (78 rpm, 10"). b) Norwegian
Office of Cultural Relations NOCR 63199 and 63200 (two 78 rpm,
12" records, whose respective second sides, NOCR 62615 and
62616, contain H. Sæverud: Galdreslåtten). c) Mercury MG 10149
(mono, with Valen: *Le Cimetière Marin* and *La Isla de las Calmas*,
and three works by H. Sæverud).

SONETTO DI MICHELANGELO. Miltiades Caridis, [Oslo] Philharmonic Society Orc. See *Pastorale*.

NENIA. Miltiades Caridis, [Oslo] Philharmonic Society Orc. See *Pastorale*.

CANTICO DI RINGRAZIAMENTO. Miltiades Caridis, [Oslo] Philharmonic Society Orc. See *Pastorale*.

AN DIE HOFFNUNG. Miltiades Caridis, [Oslo] Philharmonic Society Orc. See *Pastorale*.

EPITHALAMION. Karsten Andersen, [Bergen] Harmonien Orc. Philips 6507 039 (with Valen: Concerto for Violin and Orchestra (Arve Tellefsen, violin; same conductor and orchestra) and Trio (Stig Nilsson, violin; Hege Waldeland, cello; Eva Knardahl, piano)).

LE CIMETIÈRE MARIN. Øivin Fjeldstad, [Oslo] Philharmonic Society Orc. a) Musica SK 15542 (78 rpm, 12"). b) Norwegian Office of Cultural Relations NOCR 63156 and 63157 (two 78 rpm, 12" records, whose respective second sides, NOCR 63187 and 63188, contain Valen: *La Isla de las Calmas*). c) Mercury MG 10149 (mono, with Valen: *Sonetto di Michelangelo* and *La Isla de las Calmas*, and three works by H. Sæverud).

LE CIMETIÈRE MARIN. Miltiades Caridis, [Oslo] Philharmonic Society Orc. See *Pastorale*.

LA ISLA DE LAS CALMAS. Øivin Fjeldstad, [Oslo] Philharmonic Society Orc. a) Musica KN 7100 (78 rpm, 10"). b) Norwegian Office of Cultural Relations NOCR 63187 and 63188 (two 78 rpm, 12" records, whose respective second sides, NOCR 63156 and 63157, contain Valen: *Le Cimetière Marin*). c) Mercury MG 10149 (mono, with Valen: *Sonetto di Michelangelo* and *Le Cimetière Marin*, and three works by H. Sæverud).

LA ISLA DE LAS CALMAS. Miltiades Caridis, [Oslo] Philharmonic Society Orc. See *Pastorale*.

ODE TIL ENSOMHETEN. Miltiades Caridis, [Oslo] Philharmonic Society Orc. See *Pastorale*.

ORCHESTRAL AUTOGRAPH MANUSCRIPTS

Nearly all of these are in the Norwegian Music Collection of the University of Oslo library. Their use is subject to restrictions mentioned in this chapter.

SELECTED WRITINGS BY FARTEIN VALEN

[with Torstein Gunnarson:] "I samtale med Fartein Valen", in *Norsk Musikktidsskrift*, vol. 4 no. 1, Mar. 1967; pp. 12-15.

"Et ungdomsbrev fra Fartein Valen", in *Norsk Musikktidsskrift*, vol. 6 no. 3, Sep. 1969; pp. 112-13, 115.

[with Else Christie Kielland:] "Selvbiografiske data", in *Norsk Musikktidsskrift*, vol. 6 no. 4, Dec. 1969; pp. 164-66.

SELECTED WRITINGS BY OTHERS ABOUT VALEN

Olav Gurvin: "Fartein Valen", in his *Frå Tonalitet til Atonalitet* (Oslo: H. Aschehoug, 1938); pp. 62-83.

Olav Gurvin: *Fartein Valen—En Banebryter i Nyere Norsk Musikk* (Drammen: Harald Lyche, 1962).

Bjarne Kortsen: *Gjennom Kamp til Seier—Førstefremføringer av Fartein Valens Musikk i Norsk Presse gjennom Ca. 40 År* (Oslo: Bjarne Kortsen, 1963).

Bjarne Kortsen: *Melodic Structure and Thematic Unity in Fartein Valen's Music* Volumes 1 and 2 (Glasgow: Bjarne Kortsen, 1963).

Bjarne Kortsen: *Fartein Valen: Life and Music* Volumes 1, 2, and 3 (Oslo: Johan Grundt Tanum, 1965).

Bjarne Kortsen: *Utgivelsen av Fartein Valens Klaverkonsert Op. 44* (Bergen: Bjarne Kortsen, 1971).

Anon.: *Komponisten Fartein Valen 1887-1952* (Oslo: Fartein Valen Selskapet, 1976).

Kaikhosru Shapurji Sorabji in about 1934

VII   Kaikhosru Shapurji Sorabji and his *Opus Clavicembalisticum*

Why do I write as I do? Why did (and do) the artists-craftsmen of Iran, India, China, Byzantine-Arabic Sicily (in the first and last of which are my own ancestral roots) produce the sort of elaborate highly wrought work they did? That was their way. It is also mine. If you don't like it, because it isn't the present-day done thing, that is too bad, but not for me, who couldn't care less. In fact, to me your disapproval is an indirect compliment and much less of an insult than your applause, when I consider some of your idols.[1]

As has been said recently, Kaikhosru Shapurji Sorabji *may* have been born in Chingford, Essex on 14 August 1892. Other dates and places have been suggested, not least by Sorabji himself: he considers that any enquiries into private matters deserve either no reply or a deliberately misleading one. For the most part, he has kept details of his personal life hidden, and he has spoken out against many public descriptions of himself. Nothing infuriates him more than to be described as an "Indian composer".[2] He considers his true paternal ancestry Persian. His father was indeed a Parsi, a member of that small, wealthy, elite, and influential group of Indians whose Zoroastrian ancestors left Persia for India in the seventh century because of the invading Moslems. His mother he describes as a Spanish-Sicilian. But "Parsi composer" and "Sicilian composer" are of little use, and as to "British composer", Sorabji once wrote a typically defiant and elaborate rejection of it which begins as follows:

> English law, with a perverse and original oddity recalling the "mad Englishman" of the eighteenth century — that stimulating and engaging eccentric that this land used to produce when it was still inhabited by individuals, rather than the members of a cinema audience, and when a capacity to think and feel for themselves had not been roller-milled out of them by an educational process

which leaves them with the correct ideas about everything and the right ideas about nothing — English law decrees that a kitten born in a kennel is a puppy, a piglet born in a stable a horse.[3]

In other words, as he goes on to explain, his mere birth and presence in Britain do not make him a British composer, especially since his ancestry, attitudes, and music are very un-British, and since he has for years been *persona ingratissima*[4] in British musical life. "British composer" implies more than "writer of music born or working in Britain"; it is those further implications which he objects to.

He was privately educated and began composing shortly before the first world war. His first important published writing about music dates from the time of that war. He was a frequent contributor to *The Sackbut* in its first year (1920-21). From 1924 to 1934 he was a regular music reviewer for *The New Age*, and from 1932 to 1945 for *The New English Weekly*. *The Sackbut* was founded as a monthly and run for a short time by Philip Heseltine (Peter Warlock). The other two publications were weeklies edited at the time (until his death in 1934) by Alfred Richard Orage, an enthusiast of Clifford Douglas's theories of social credit economics. Between 1915 and 1949 Sorabji contributed 572 items to these two journals: 499 articles and reviews plus 73 letters. His opinions on non-musical matters as expressed at that time are important for a fuller understanding of him: for example, his own pro-social-credit position, his pro-abortion position in 1929, his pro-Italian position in the early 1930's, and his anti-American position generally. By far most of his writing, however, is on musical subjects. But regardless of subject, he very often expresses himself in extremes notable for their density and quality of extravagant metaphor, panegyric paean, and corrosive condemnation. Two examples follow.[5]

Around this poem, Szymanowski has written music of a radiant purity of spirit, of an elevated ecstasy of expression, music so permeated with the very essence of the choicest and rarest specimens of Iranian art — the whole score glows with gorgeous colour, rich, yet never garish nor crude, like a Persian painting or silk rug — that such a feat is unparalleled in Western music . . . The score of the *Third Symphony* is a marvel — firm in structure and essen-

KAIKHOSRU SHAPURJI SORABJI   163

tial cohesion, yet disembodied and transparent as gossamer; glowing with the utmost of scintillant luminosity, yet rich in deep dark velvety shadows, elevated and lofty in expression, yet without a hint of magniloquence, pomposity, or the striking of attitudes . . .

Prout, as one might expect, displayed in his "compositions" — if those unbelievably feeble and jejune recollections of watered Mendelssohn and second-hand Haydn can be so called — a combination of *naiveté*, ineptitude and sheer incompetence that have to be seen to be believed. Not one single flash, one sparklet of character, invention or even pleasantly ingenious joinery enlivens or adds interest, even the most transient, to these aborted jellyfish.

Sorabji had a great dislike for some contemporary composers — such as Holst, Stravinsky, Shostakovich, Hindemith, twelve-tone Schoenberg, Webern, and most of Bartók. Equally great was his approval of other contemporaries, many of whom were "outsiders" like himself: Rachmaninov, Medtner, Szymanowski, Heseltine, Delius, van Dieren, Francis George Scott, and Busoni. Busoni was a particular favourite: Sorabji sees Busoni's musical philosophies, performing, and compositions as having meant more to him than those of any other contemporary musician. Sorabji performed his own piano music for Busoni in 1919, after which Busoni wrote him an open letter of introduction. Busoni's piano student, Egon Petri, gained exceedingly high praise from Sorabji nearly every time he played in London from 1925 to the second world war. It was probably Petri's playing of Busoni's *Fantasia Contrappuntistica* in the late 1920's which gave Sorabji an impetus for the writing of his *Opus Clavicembalisticum*, Petri's playing of Liszt's twelve transcendental studies which led to Sorabji's 100 transcendental studies, and Petri's playing of Busoni's transcription of Bach's Chromatic Fantasy and Fugue which led to Sorabji's own transcription of the same work.

Sorabji's chief compositions comprise about 35 works for solo piano (including the three works just mentioned), three for organ, eight for piano and orchestra, six others involving orchestra (including some with voices), and five sets of songs. In the 1920's and 1930's he occasionally played some of his solo piano works in public. Between 1921 and 1931, 15 of his compositions were published, chiefly at his own or his

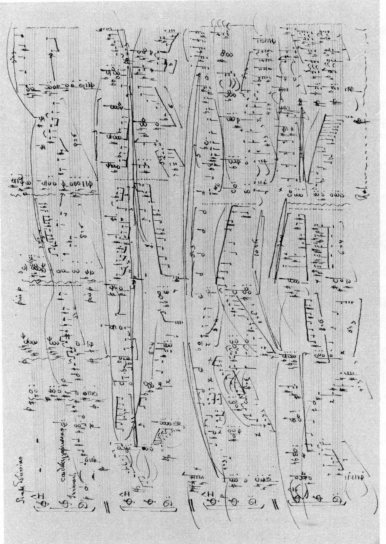

Page 154 of Sorabji's autograph manuscript of
Opus Clavicembalisticum (from the Adagio of
Interlude II)

family's expense. But 1931 was the last year his music was published, with one small and interesting exception, and 1936 was the last year he gave a public concert. He had had enough of audiences, critics, concert managers, performers, etc., most of whom he found offensively unintelligent, dull, unmusical, and unwilling and unable to understand him. In his book *Mi Contra Fa*, published in 1947, he explained his "reasons for not going to concerts" (he still went, but much less often than before), "reasons for having nothing to do with musicians", and "reasons for living in a granite tower" — not a traditional ivory tower,

> but a Tower of Granite with plentiful supplies of boiling oil and molten lead handy to tip over the battlements on to the heads of unwanted and uninvited intruders on my privacy and seclusion.[6]

Probably in 1936 or 1937, Sorabji also decided that there would be no more public performances of his works by anyone. Having retained the copyright on all his published music, he felt quite able to institute this unofficial ban. An unacceptable performance of part of his *Opus Clavicembalisticum* in March 1936 by John Tobin was one of the last in a series of incidents leading to the ban. He reasoned that the inablility of performers and listeners to play and understand his music made a total lack of performances preferable to taking further chances with mediocre ones or worse. Public performances by others under ideal circumstances probably remained for him a remote possibility, but basically he determined that henceforth he would be composing and performing for select individuals in private situations. That was the only way his music could be heard with everything under his control.

After December 1936 there were no authorized public performances of Sorabji's music and very few unauthorized ones. There is a reason for this besides the ban: the music itself. The harmonic complexity, ornamental profusion, extreme length, and overwhelming technical difficulties of most of his works would and did turn away many potential performers. The aspect of length is the easiest to illustrate: about ten of the works for solo piano and several for other forces take up an entire programme and probably last two hours or more.

His predilection for the enormous may seem abnormal in the west, but in classical Persian and Indian music, for example, performances of an evening's duration have not been so unusual. Furthermore, Sorabji seems to have been fascinated by the profusion of detail and the improvisational nature of some of the elaborate ornamentation of eastern art, music included. His music may also have been affected by the sort of metric organization, freer than in most western tonal music, to be found in some Indian and Persian classical music. Sorabji's music, while almost always tonal, even if in rather expanded senses of that term, rarely falls into regular patterns of meter and phrasing. Even in the massive fugues which form part of many keyboard works and which have a regular pulse, meter follows phrasing, tonality is elusive, and subjects are treated quite freely.

He continued to review concerts and records regularly for nearly nine years after he stopped performing. He was under no financial pressure to do so, as the money left him by his father after his death in 1932 made it unnecessary for him to have to work for a living.

Despite his fondness for gramophone records as a way to present music without the uncertainties and fallibilities of live concerts, he has never made any records himself. In 1936, partly as a result of Tobin's performance and some unfavourable reviews it received, requests poured in to *The New English Weekly* from as far away as California to have Sorabji record his own music. He refused, citing inadequacies in the copyright laws, which allow anyone paying or tendering a fee to record something, however badly, if it has been recorded once already. In 1953 many admirers of Sorabji, including well-known people such as Egon Petri, Osbert Sitwell, Clinton Gray-Fisk, and John Ireland, presented him with a tape recorder, possibly with hopes that he would record something on his own which could be distributed privately as a tape or record. Professionally made recordings may also have been discussed, as Sorabji's longtime friend Frank Holliday recalls that Sorabji was averse to the idea then and afterwards of either transporting his unique Steinway grand piano to a recording studio or having recording engineers come into and disrupt his home. In any case, the difficult last illness of

Sorabji's mother made any recording scheme impossible.

Another reason for his refusal to record, and for that matter his stopping to perform, may have been that he did not consider himself able to play his music up to his own high standards, at least not in public. He has always said that he has no great pretensions as a pianist. This is not likely false modesty, for there is little of that in Sorabji. (In fact, any evaluation by him in print of his own playing or compositions is very rare.) Other people may have said he was one of only few who could do his piano music justice in performance, but *he* never said that, despite his dissatisfaction with most pianists.

There are two sources of information about Sorabji's manner of playing his own music. Neither answers questions about performance which the scores themselves pose.

The first source is statements by witnesses of Sorabji's performances. Most are too general to be of any real value. Of several reviews, only a few seem written by persons who made an attempt to understand the music. Of these, three stand out in quality: reviews in *The Glasgow Herald* of Sorabji's concerts in Glasgow in 1930 and 1936[7] under the auspices of the Active Society for the Propagation of Contemporary Music, whose founder and director was Sorabji's friend Erik Chisholm. The three reviews were probably written by the same person; at least, whoever wrote the second and the third reviews seems to have been present at Sorabji's earlier concert(s). The reviews all remark that Sorabji tended to play impatiently and with little contrast among sections whose titles or programme-note descriptions suggested considerable difference of character and treatment.

The second source of information is a group of six tape recordings Sorabji made of some of his piano works. They were recorded by Frank Holliday at Sorabji's residence in Dorset in 1962, 63, 64, 65, and 68. Very short excerpts from them were used in a talk titled "The Composer Sorabji" written and taped by Erik Chisholm shortly before his death in 1965. Chisholm apparently considered his talk not suitable for further use, as he asked Frank Holliday to rerecord it. The resultant product, Chisholm's talk edited, read, and introduced by Frank Holliday with excerpts from the performances by Sorabji, was first broadcast in New York in December 1969. Subsequently, Sorabji's American friend Donald Garvelmann taped a two-and-a-half-hour radio programme consisting of his own remarks, the complete Chisholm-Holliday talk, and Sorabji's complete performance of two of his piano works. This programme was first broadcast in 1970, also in New York, and has since been heard in several parts of the U.S.A.[8]

The tapes seem of little value in determining how Sorabji might have played his music decades ago, or how he might want it played now. They were made under difficult conditions and when he was no longer young. The variance in every parameter between the scores and the performances is enormous, and the playing itself is quite casual. Curiously, the impression of his playing on the broadcast recordings is similar to that mentioned by the Glasgow reviewer(s), especially in the slight differentiation given to music which on paper demands more.[9] Sorabji's brilliance as a performer of his own music is mentioned by several reviewers and by friends who have heard him play, publicly or privately, but it is hinted at only rarely in the broadcast material. It is indeed unfortunate that he made no recordings in the 1930's.

In the course of the 40-year ban on performances of his music, there were some requests by pianists to have it broken in their favour. Sorabji's refusals resulted as much from disgust with contemporary musical life in Britain as from distrust of any particular pianist's abilities. It was thus a shock to those who knew him and his music well to learn in the spring of 1976 that Yonty Solomon had been given permission to play whatever compositions for solo piano he wanted wherever he wanted, especially as Solomon had been refused before. The explanation lies partly in the fact that Sorabji's close friend Alistair Hinton, whose judgement he trusted completely in this matter, recommended Solomon to him. Sorabji also learned that Solomon had been a favourite pupil of Erik Chisholm. On 7 December 1976, 40 years less nine days after the last authorized performance of Sorabji's music, Yonty Solomon included four short works, all published in the 1920's, in a concert in the Wigmore Hall, London. Shortly afterwards he taped them, with Sorabji's permission, for broadcast by the B.B.C. This broke another ban, as the B.B.C. had not been permitted to broadcast the Chisholm-Holliday or Garvelmann programmes or anything else concerning Sorabji over which Sorabji had control. Solomon then made plans to perform *Opus Clavicembalisticum* (henceforth *O.C.*) in 1977. He already knew most of this score, the largest by Sorabji to have been published, from having studied it for a number of years.

In early 1977, it was learned that Sorabji had also given permission (in 1975) to Michael Habermann for performances in the U.S.A. This permission was also granted through a friend of Sorabji's, in this case Donald Garvelmann. Although Sorabji's approval of Habermann appears to have predated his approval of Solomon, Habermann's first public performance of Sorabji's music, also of short, early works, took place after Solomon's, on 22 May 1977. Yonty Solomon played the first big composition by Sorabji to be heard since 1936, the Sonata No. 3, on 16 June 1977.[10]

O.C. was written in 1929-30. It is 248 pages of music in the approximately 13" x 10" published format, and 253 pages in Sorabji's manuscript of similar dimensions. It is divided into three large parts of twelve sections altogether, with an interval possible after parts I and II (although neither score, i.e. print or manuscript, suggests a break anywhere in the music). Its total length without intervals is said to be over two and a half hours. The sections are as follows. In the score, all the titles are in Italian or Latin.[11]

Part I	1. Introit
	2. Chorale Prelude
	3. Fugue [No.] I [with 1 subject]
	4. Fantasia
	5. Fugue [No. II] with 2 subjects [subsections 5a and 5b]
Part II	6. Interlude I: theme and 49 variations[12]
	7. Cadenza I
	8. Fugue [No. III] with 3 subjects [subsections 8a, 8b, 8c]
Part III	9. Interlude II: toccata [9a], adagio [9b], and passacaglia with 81 variations [9c]
	10. Cadenza II
	11. Fugue [No. IV] with 4 subjects [subsections 11a, 11b, 11c, 11d]
	12. Coda Stretta

Sorabji gave the first performance (complete) at one of Chisholm's Glasgow concerts on 1 December 1930. On 10 March 1936, Tobin played Part I, but according to one reviewer who knew Sorabji (Edward Clarke Ashworth, writing in *The New English Weekly*), he played it poorly and took about twice as long to get through it as he should have. Sorabji later explained that rumours that he financed this concert were monstrously false, and that when told of arrangements for the concert he disapproved, but

> I was only restrained from imposing my veto by a desire not to cause loss or inconvenience to those concerned, and I refused to be associated with the occasion or to endorse it by being present.[13]

From the time of its first performance in 1930 and its publication in 1931, *O.C.* became Sorabji's most discussed work. It soon came to be called the longest piano solo in existence, which it is not, and which in any case it could not possibly be verified as being.

The dedication to Christopher Murray Grieve (Hugh MacDiarmid) is a colourful elaboration of the idea contained in the last two sentences of the opening quotation in this chapter:

> to my two friends (e duobus unum):
> Hugh M'Diarmid
> and
> C.M. Grieve
> likewise
> to the everlasting glory of those few
> men
> blessed and sanctified in the
> curses and execrations of those
> many
> whose praise is eternal damnation
>
> June MCMXXX

Sorabji gave his autograph manuscript to Erik Chisholm at Christmastime 1931. When Chisholm died, after teaching music for many years at the University of Cape Town, the manuscript went to that university's library, where it remains

At the end of the manuscript is a solemn Latin inscription which is printed in the published score, except for the last phrase, which provides a certain link to the sentiments expressed at the end of the dedication. The full inscription translates as follows:

† In the name of the father, the son, and the holy ghost: at 1.50 p.m. on the 25th day of the month of June 1930 A.D.N.S., Kaikhosru Sorabji completed this composition at his home, 1175 Clarence Gate [should read: 175 Clarence Gate Gardens], district of Regent's Park, London, amidst the most barbaric and crapulous Britons.

Sorabji's twelve main section titles suggest a debt to the baroque which is confirmed by the music itself. They also suggest the immediate antecedent of at least the plan of the whole work, Busoni's *Fantasia Contrappuntistica*. Busoni's work and *O.C.* both have the same number of sections; both have a chorale prelude near or at the beginning and a stretto section at the end; the terms for other sections of both are similar or identical; both have four fugues. The original title of *O.C.* was actually *Opus Sequentiale*, which referred specifically to the sequence of four fugues which it is built around.

Sorabji lists 24 different melodic themes in a table at the end of the manuscript of *O.C.* Sixteen are fugue subjects or countersubjects (found in sections 3, 5, 8, and 11); one theme each is given for the fantasia (section 4), first interlude (section 6), and passacaglia of the second interlude (subsection 9c); and five are given for the introit (section 1). The remaining full sections, along with subsections 9a and 9b, use previously heard themes or variants of them. Later subsections of individual fugues also use themes from earlier subsections of the same fugue, and fugues II and III use themes from fugue I and from fugues I and II respectively.

Further thematic unity is provided by the motto theme, heard unaccompanied at the very beginning of *O.C.* (see ex. 1).[14] Typical of all the themes of *O.C.* is the freedom with which they are treated, and none is recalled in more varied shapes than this motto theme: see exs. 2 to 6, which are from (in order) sections 2 and 3 and subsections 9a, 9b, and 9c. Exs. 4 and 5 make use of the six-note descent at the end of

ex. 1, ex. 5 extending it into a very long inversion. Ex. 6, the
passacaglia theme, may at first seem unrelated to ex. 1. But
both consist of three descents symmetrically surrounding two
ascents (see ex. 7), with the *descending skips* and *ascending
steps* of ex. 1 becoming respectively the *descending steps* and
ascending skips of ex. 6.

Exs. 8 and 9 are two more themes from the introit. They
too are derivable from ex. 1, but more obscurely, and via two
further themes which are not shown. Exs. 8 and 9, which are
really variants of each other, are set up in an antecedent-con-
sequent relationship which is sometimes broken up in the introit and the chorale prelude. This relationship is reconsti-
tuted much later, in the first interlude (section 6), whose variations' theme (ex. 10) is a further inflection of exs. 8 and 9.

The nonfugal and nonvariational portions of *O.C.* (i.e. nos.
1, 2, 4, 7, 9a, 9b, and 10) are constructed freely, without reference to any well-known form pattern. They consist chiefly
of elaborate and richly varied ornamentations of various
themes of the work. The themes themselves are not *developed*
in the usual sonata-form sense of the term. There is plenty of
dramatic action in these sections, but it is not the result of
the dualism of themes or tonalities of the classical sonata, nor
of the opposition of statement and development in a general
sense, nor of sudden or extreme changes in the style of the
music. Pace and tension are controlled more by the type of
ornamentation; its speed, register, dynamics, timbre, rhythmic
combinations, texture, overall gesture; and the interrelation-
ships and relatively slow changes among these things. Register,
timbre, and type and density of texture are particularly important in defining the progress and form of these portions,
while traditionally primary factors such as surface harmonic
motion are less important. Even determining which theme is
being ornamented in a particular passage is at times a lesser
concern. The ornamentation tends to take over from the more
thematic material and become the focus of the activity and
expression. The varieties of ornamentation are very numerous,
from the simple running 16th notes at the beginning of sec-
ions 7 and 9 (see ex. 11, from subsection 9a), to the vehement
chordal formations all over the keyboard at the end of sections 4 and 10 (see ex. 12, from section 4), to various kinds

of free, irregular counterpoint in many voices with no strong pulse (see ex. 13, from subsection 9b).

The most elaborate example of the last-mentioned is the *adagio* subsection 9b, a calm, floating music which is no louder than *mp* over its whole ten minutes' duration until the final solemn procession of 36 chords right down the keyboard from an initial *ppp* to a final *ff*. Most of this subsection contains only dream-images of themes. The complex proportional rhythmic ornamentation is often nearly impossible to play literally, which fortunately seems undesirable anyway. The frequent indications of 12=7, 11=8, 5=3, etc. (often simultaneous with no common factor) are probably guides to flexibly articulated note groupings rather than indicators of equal divisions of pulses.

The sense of the "free-form" portions of *O.C.* is thus of groups of written-out improvisations. Exact determination of all the smallest details is relatively unimportant. This also links *O.C.* to various eastern musics rather than to most well-known western cultivated music. A very few aspects are compositionally fixed, while the composition of everything else is much freer.[15] The relationship of the fixed to the free on many levels helps create the large-scale form of the whole.

Considerable freedom is to be found in the two variation sets of *O.C.*, section 6 and subsection 9c. The theme of section 6 (ex. 10) is treated extremely freely, with notes added to and omitted from the melodic line, pitches and rhythms altered in other ways, and the bipartite structural implications frequently ignored. The theme itself is sometimes heard in inversion (e.g. variations 10 and 15), sometimes preceded or followed by nonthematic material within a variation (e.g. variations 20 and 49), sometimes completely consumed by the ornamentation (e.g. variations 26 and 27). Verbal markings for some of the variations show that Sorabji is thinking well beyond the limits of his own piano (all the following indications are in Italian): "sonority like full organ with reserved expression" (variation 19), "Paganini-like" (variation 20), "Aeolian harp" (variation 22), and "the whole delicately melodious but *not* with infantilistic simpleness" (variation 39).

Section 9's variations (subsection 9c) are stricter, with the theme (ex. 6) undergoing few changes other than chordal additions to each note. Thus, in contrast to section 6, the theme of subsection 9c occurs in nearly every variation with the same pitch classes and contours and the same rhythmic proportions. The published score and autograph manuscript together suggest that the printer and Sorabji both made easily correctable errors in a number of variations. Only variations 2, 33, and 76 contain substantive rhythmic or pitch alterations to the theme. These also seem to be errors, but they can not be corrected without recomposing the music and should rather be left as they are.

Subsection 9c contains the same almost bewildering variety of ornamentation as section 6, from strict canon to the style explored in subsection 9b. Both sets of variations have a similar gradual buildup from simple to complex and from quiet to loud variations. Both sets have the same lack of overlap between adjacent variations: each variation is nearly always quite different from its neighbours. Both have rare direct references to the east: the Aeolian harp variation already mentioned and variation 53 in subsection 9c, which is marked (in Italian) "like a tambura: nostalgic, very mellow, and hypnotic". Both sets also function as units midway in stylistic and formal freedom between the two extremes of the "free-form" portions on the one hand and the fugues on the other.

Each fugue has one principal subject associated with each subsection. The ten fugal subsections reveal a general three-part plan for each. The first part, which is by far the longest, is an introduction and elaboration in four or five voices [16] of each form in turn of all four forms of the new subject (prime, retrograde, inversion, retrograde inversion – henceforth P, R, I, RI), [17] with use of countersubjects and previous subjects possible. The second part is a stretto passage and is relatively short, as is the third, a forceful climax in six voices with phrasing controlled by augmentation and some individual voices becoming chordal. Most often, the stretto and augmentation are of the particular subsection's own subject. Exceptions include F_{III-2} (i.e. fugue III, subsection 2), where the stretto passage is based on S_{III-1} (i.e. the subject first heard in F_{III-1}); and F_{IV-2}, where the augmentation is based on S_{IV-1}.

Within the basic three-part design, there are considerable differences across fugues. Some have big climaxes before the last climax; some have stretto passages in many places, on countersubjects as well as subjects; some make greater use than others of augmentation and diminution, inside and outside the third part.

Some unusual features in the stretto usage are particularly interesting and characteristic of the free approach to large-scale form which the fugues as a whole reveal. F_{III-1} includes some six-voice stretto *after* the initial augmentation part is begun. In F_{IV-1} the stretto passage on S_{IV-1} is preceded by one on CS_{IV-1}. F_{III-3} contains not one or two but 16 consecutive strettos on S_{III-3}, essentially four four-voice canons in invertible counterpoint on each of the four forms, in the order P (x4), R (x4), I (x4), RI (x4).

In all, there are ten subjects and six countersubjects (two countersubjects in F_I, one each in F_{II-1}, F_{III-1}, F_{III-2}, F_{IV-1}). The countersubjects are used a great deal, often (as has been suggested) not accompanied by the subjects they were first associated with, nor by any other thematic material. But on the whole, they are used less than the subjects, their pitch contours are smoother, and they have less rhythmic variety. Unlike all the subjects, they are not found in R and RI forms.

Some of the fugue themes, both subjects and countersubjects, are related in various ways to themes from the introit. Most of them, like the other themes of *O.C.*, emphasize scalar shapes of quasi-tonal kinds; their key centres are suggested more than defined and are of only minor structural importance. Most of the fugue themes are also extraordinarily long by renaissance and baroque standards. As a result or perhaps cause of this, the fugues themselves are long: the shortest (F_I) lasts about 15 minutes and the longest (F_{IV}) over 40. Each fugue progresses primarily by presenting the several available forms of its themes (P, R, I, RI) in many of the possible combinations of invertible counterpoint. As stated before, later subsections of a fugue make generous use of themes from earlier subsections of the same fugue, and two fugues use themes previously heard in other fugues. This naturally increases the contrapuntal possibilities immensely.

Most interestingly, there is very little development by episode, i.e. by fragments of themes or by nonthematic material.[18] Sorabji prefers to use theme statements as entire as possible throughout the course of the first two parts of the three-part design. Only in the climactic part controlled by augmentation does he regularly increase the rate of events by means of thematic fragmentation, sequence, and derived material.

The long first part of the fugue subsections, the introduction and elaboration of subjects, tends to move in very long phrases, with not as much overlap between them as might be expected. This is partly the result (or again, perhaps the cause) of all the themes in any one fugue being the same length. Sorabji may thus begin together statements of any two or more subjects or countersubjects from the same fugue and have them end together as well. An exception occurs with F_{III-1}, whose subject and countersubject are each two beats shorter than the themes of the other subsections of F_{III}. This leads to some *ad hoc* alterations to themes, made mostly in the middle and end portions of whichever forms they are used in, in order to leave the heads intact.

These alterations are very much in keeping with the freedom of treatment or relatively unfixed nature of the themes from all the fugues. All are thereby lent a certain improvisational quality beyond what is implied by the term *fugue* itself. But in comparison with, for example, the fantasia or cadenza sections of *O.C.*, they could scarcely be considered improvisational at all.

The most radical alterations on a fugue subject are those made on the head of S_I. The whole subject is given as ex. 14. In some of its occurrences in the I and RI forms, the two changes of direction in the subject (involving the third and fourth notes of the P form) are removed: see exs. 15 (I form) and 16 (RI form). There are several possible reasons for this. Perhaps Sorabji merely preferred to keep the P form's descending half-step between the second and third notes intact in the I form and then used that I form's true, unidirectional retrograde for the RI.

S_I and the two countersubjects from F_I are all relatively simple as melodies. This seems deliberate: the later fugue themes in *O.C.* are much more active melodically and rhythmically. The three themes of F_I are also fairly similar to each other; this relationship among a fugue's themes also changes later. Exs. 17 and 18 give S_{IV-3} and S_{IV-4}. Their radically different surfaces, those of the other themes of F_{IV}, and the fugal combinations created out of this diversity make this fugue a profound compositional display of amazing scope.

The twelfth section of *O.C.*, the coda stretta, acts as the climactic augmentation-controlled part to F_{IV-4} as well as coda to all of F_{IV} and all of *O.C.* In his own analytical note at the end of the manuscript, Sorabji writes "it is not till the CODA STRETTA of the whole work that themes of preceding fugues are woven into the texture". This is not true, but with reference to just F_{IV} it is (which is perhaps what Sorabji means), since up to the coda stretta, F_{IV} uses none but its own themes. Even so, most of the coda stretta is involved solely with F_{IV} material. It begins on p. 240, as in ex. 19, in seven voices proclaiming six different themes from F_{IV}. Not before p. 247 does material external to F_{IV} come in. It is here that the coda to the whole work should be considered to begin. The final six pages of *O.C.* are a virtuoso summing up, eventually making use of the motto theme (ex. 1), various themes from F_{IV}, and the subjects from the initial subsections of all four fugues.

O.C. concludes with thundering passage work, *con somma forza e grandezza*, spread across five staves. It is a shock that the composition actually ends, not really because it is so long, but because of the immensity of the artistic conception it presents. It is a still greater shock to consider, if one can, that *O.C.* is but one of many immense creations for solo piano by Sorabji — not to mention the chamber and orchestral works.

Footnotes to Chapter VII

1 Hugh MacDiarmid (Christopher Murray Grieve): *The Company I've Kept* (London: Hutchinson, 1966); p. 39.

2 as, for example, in the entry under his name written by Terence White Gervais in *Grove's Dictionary of Music and Musicians*, fifth edition (London: MacMillan, 1954); vol. 7, p. 970.

3 Kaikhosru Shapurji Sorabji: *Mi Contra Fa—The Immoralisings of a Machiavellian Musician* (London: Porcupine Press, 1947); p. 76.

4 *Ibid.*; p. 78.

5 *Ibid.*; pp. 183-84 and p. 47. Although these two quotations are from one of Sorabji's books, similar items could be quoted from his journalistic writings.

6 *Ibid.*; p. 145.

7 The reviews were printed on 2.IV.1930, 2.XII.1930, and 17.XII. 1936, in each case the day after the performance.

8 In 1969, Garvelmann published Sorabji's first pastiche on Chopin's "Minute Waltz". This is the only composition of Sorabji's to have been published since 1931. See Donald M. Garvelmann, ed.: *Thirteen Transcriptions for Piano Solo of Chopin's Waltz in D Flat, Op. 64 No. 1 (The Minute Waltz)* (Bronx, New York, U.S.A.: Music Treasure Publications, 1969), especially pp. 63-78, which contain the Sorabji pastiche, and p. 98, which reproduces part of the composer's autograph manuscript of the opening of this work.

9 I have followed nearly all the broadcast performances with copies of the scores which Sorabji presumably used. Most of these are unpublished but were microfilmed in the mid-1950's and in 1964.

10 Although he gave authorization for performances to these pianists based on the recommendations of his two friends, Sorabji did hear them play, via radio and via tape recorder, before their first concerts took place.

11 These translations are made from the material appearing under the heading "Constitution of the work" on what would be p. 2 of the published score if the page were numbered. The subsection numbering is added here for convenience.

12 A number of sources claim that this section has 44 variations, as indeed the "Constitution" page says. The "XLIV" found there is a misreading of the rather unclear "XLIX" which appears in the same place in the autograph manuscript. The music itself, of course contains 49 variations.

13   *The Musical Times*, no. 1127, vol. 78, Jan. 1937; p. 60.

14   All accidentals in these examples are valid only for the notes which
     they stand immediately in front of, and for tied notes and immedi-
     ately repeated notes (i.e. notes of the same *pitch*, not pitch class).
     Tempo and dynamics markings are often lacking in the score and
     are added in brackets only when it is fairly clear that they apply.
     Because it is not practical to count measure numbers in O.C., a
     Roman numeral is used following a page number to refer to a staff
     system on that page.

15   Compositional freedom or improvisation in construction does not,
     of course, necessarily entail any lack of architectonic form, nor any
     degree of improvisation in performance.

16   The fifth voice becomes a regular feature of this first part in sub-
     section 11c.

17   The subjects are actually introduced in the order P, R, I, RI in all
     the fugal subsections but two. The first (section 3) uses the order
     P, I, RI, R; the second (subsection 5a) uses the order P, I, R, RI. In
     the first few fugal subsections, Sorabji may have been working out
     an ideal order which, once found, was kept for the rest of O.C.

18   I am considering *episodes* here to mean passages in which virtually
     entire statements of subjects *or* countersubjects are lacking, since
     the countersubjects are often treated as independent themes in
     themselves.

Adagio

Ex. 1: Opus Clavicembalisticum (p. 5-I)

Ex. 2: Opus Clavicembalisticum (p. 18-III)

[Moderato]

Ex. 3: Opus Clavicembalisticum (p. 26-IV)

Ex. 4: Opus Clavicembalisticum (p. 137-III)

Adagio

ppp   *pp*

Ex. 5: Opus Clavicembalisticum (p. 147-IV)

Moderato

p

Ex. 6: Opus Clavicembalisticum (p. 153-II)

Ex. 1   Ex. 6

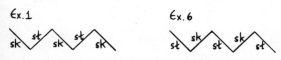

Ex. 7: Opus Clavicembalisticum (sk=skip, st=step)

Ex. 8   Ex. 9

non ◁＝＝ poco
troppo
f

Exs. 8 and 9: Opus Clavicembalisticum (p. 6-II, III)

Adagissimo

Ex. 10: Opus Clavicembalisticum (p. 59-I)

Ex. 11:   Opus Clavicembalisticum (p. 137-III)

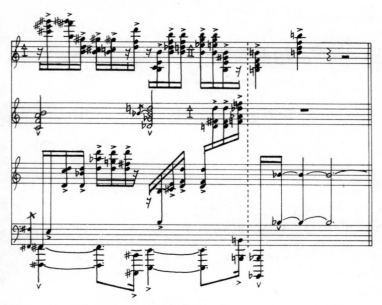

Ex. 12: Opus Clavicembalisticum (p. 39-II)

[Adagio] intensivo

Ex. 13: Opus Clavicembalisticum (p. 152-II)

Sommessamente moderato

Ex. 14: Opus Clavicembalisticum (p. 19-III)

Moderato

Ex. 15: Opus Clavicembalisticum (p. 24-II)

[Moderato]

Ex. 16: Opus Clavicembalisticum (p. 25-II, III)

Severo, didattico

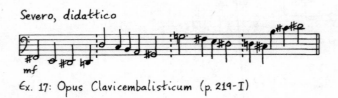

Ex. 17: Opus Clavicembalisticum (p. 219-I)

Irato impaziente

Ex. 18: Opus Clavicembalisticum (p. 229-II, III)

Quasi organo pieno

Ex. 19: Opus Clavicembalisticum (p. 240-III)

SOLO PIANO WORKS BY KAIKHOSRU SHAPURJI SORABJI

For an explanation of abbreviations and what is included in this list, see page 19.

Note: Oxford University Press has had the selling rights for some time to all the works published between 1921 and 1931.

QUASI HABANERA (1917)

TWO PIANO PIECES: IN THE HOTHOUSE (1918)
                   TOCCATA (1920)
    Pbd: London. London and Continental Music Publishing, 1921.

FANTAISIE ESPAGNOLE (1919)
    Pbd: London. London and Continental Music Publishing, 1922.

SONATA NO. 1 (1919)
    Pbd: London. London and Continental Music Publishing, 1921.

PRELUDE, INTERLUDE, AND FUGUE (1920-22)
    Pbd: London. J. Curwen and Sons, 1924.

SONATA NO. 2 (1920)
    Pbd: London. F. and B. Goodwin, 1923.

SONATA NO. 3 (1922)
    1st prf: 16.VI.1977, by Yonty Solomon.
    Pbd: London. J. Curwen and Sons, 1924.

THREE PASTICHES (1922): on Chopin's *Minute Waltz* (in D♭ major, op. 64 no. 1);
                   on Bizet's *Habanera* (from *Carmen*);
                   on Rimskiy-Korsakov's *Hindu Merchant's Song* (from *Sadko*)
    Pbd: (Chopin pastiche only) Bronx, New York, U.S.A. Music Treasure Publications, 1969.

LE JARDIN PARFUMÉ, *Poem for Piano* (1923)
    Pbd: London. J. Curwen and Sons, 1927.

VARIATIONS AND FUGUE ON "DIES IRAE" (1923-26)

VALSE-FANTAISIE, *Hommage à Johann Strauss* (1925)
    Pbd: London. J. Curwen and Sons, 1927.

FRAGMENT (1926, rev. 37)
    1st prf: 12.X.1927, by Harold Rutland.

TOCCATA NO. 1 (1928)

NOCTURNE, *Jāmī* (1928)
?1st prf: 29.IV.1931, by Kaikhosru Shapurji Sorabji.

SONATA NO. 4 (1928-29)
1st prf: 1.IV.1930, by Kaikhosru Shapurji Sorabji.

OPUS CLAVICEMBALISTICUM (1929-30)
1st prf: 1.XII.1930, by Kaikhosru Shapurji Sorabji.
Pbd: London. J. Curwen and Sons, 1931.

FANTASIA ISPANICA (1933)

CAPRICE-PASTICHE ON OP. 64 NO. 1 OF CHOPIN [the *Minute Waltz*] (1933)

TOCCATA NO. 2 (1933-34)
1st prf: 16.XII.1936, by Kaikhosru Shapurji Sorabji.

SONATA NO. 5, *Opus Archimagicum* (1934-35)

SYMPHONIC VARIATIONS (1935-37)

TANTRIK SYMPHONY [Symphony No. 1] (1938-39)

TRANSCRIPTION IN THE LIGHT OF HARPSICHORD TECHNIQUE FOR THE MODERN PIANO OF *The Chromatic Fantasia* OF J.S. BACH, FOLLOWED BY A [DIFFERENT] FUGUE (1940)

"QUAERE RELIQUA HUJUS MATERIEI INTER SECRETIORA" (1940)

"GULISTAN", *Nocturne for Piano* (1940)

[100] TRANSCENDENTAL STUDIES (1940-44)

ST. BERTRAND DE COMMINGES: "HE WAS LAUGHING IN THE TOWER" (1941)

CONCERT TRANSCRIPTION OF RAVEL'S *Rapsodie Espagnole* (1945)

CONCERTO PER SUONARE DA ME SOLO, E SENZA ORCHESTRA, PER DIVERTIRSI (1946)

CONCERT PARAPHRASE OF THE CLOSING SCENE FROM R. STRAUSS'S *Salome* (1947)

SEQUENTIA CYCLICA SUPER "DIES IRAE" EX *Missa pro Defunctis*, IN CLAVICEMBALI USUM (1948-49)

SYMPHONY NO. 2 (1954)

PASSEGGIATA VENEZIANA (1956)

SYMPHONY NO. 3 (1959-60)

FRAMMENTI AFORISTICI (1962 et seq.)

SYMPHONY NO. 4 (1962-64)

TOCCATA NO. 4 (1964-67)

SYMPHONY NO. 5, *Symphonia Brevis* (1973)

SYMPHONY NO. 6, *Symphonia Magna* (1975-76)

FRAMMENTI AFORISTICI (1977)

Note: Two works could not have their dates of composition determined, FANTASIETTINA ON THE NAME H.McD./C.M.G. and ROSARIO D'ARABESCHI.

OTHER WORKS

three organ symphonies (1924, 1929-32, 1949-53); eight works for piano and orchestra; two works for orchestra without voices; two symphonies for piano, organ, chorus, and orchestra (1921-22, 1942-51; the second, *Jāmī*, also uses a baritone solo); Symphonic High Mass (1955-61); two piano quintets (1920, 1932-33); many songs.

DISCOGRAPHY

No commercial records have been made of Sorabji's music.

SOLO PIANO AUTOGRAPH MANUSCRIPTS

Most of these are with the composer. Many are on microfilm at the libraries of the University of Cape Town and of Northwestern University, Evanston, Illinois, U.S.A.

SELECTED WRITINGS BY KAIKHOSRU SHAPURJI SORABJI

"Modern piano technique", in *The Sackbut*, vol. 1 no. 3, July 1920; pp. 116-23.

"Music. The passing of the public concert" parts I and II, in *The New Age*, nos. 1765-66, vol. 39 nos. 11-12, 8. and 15.VII.1926; pp. 110 and 121-22.

"Music . . ." [on gramophones and their salesmen], in *The New Age*, no. 1836, vol. 42 no. 3, 17.XI.1927; pp. 32-33.

" 'Le Jardin Parfumé' ", in *The Musical Times*, no. 1030, vol. 69, 1.XII. 1928; p. 799.

"Music. Bartók recital . . . Hallé concert. The Musical Copyright bill", in *The New Age*, no. 1950, vol. 46 no. 12, 23.I.1930; p. 137.

Around Music (London: Unicorn Press, 1932).

"Music" [on gramophone music heard in India and some Richard Tauber records], in *The New Age*, no. 2102, vol. 52 no. 8, 22.XII. 1932; p. 92.

"Music. The Busoni concerto . . . Egon Petri recital . . .", in *The New English Weekly*, vol. 4 no. 21, 8.III.1934; pp. 495-96.

"Opus Clavicembalisticum", in *The New English Weekly*, vol. 9 no. 22, 10.IX.1936; p. 360.

"Music. Busoni's 'Doktor Faust' ", in *The New English Weekly*, vol. 10 no. 25, 1.IV.1937; pp. 494-96.

Mi Contra Fa—The Immoralisings of a Machiavellian Musician (London: Porcupine Press, 1947).

"The validity of the aristocratic principle", in K. Bharatha Iyer, ed.: *Art and Thought* (London: Luzac, 1947); pp. 214-18.

"The greatness of Medtner", in Richard Holt, ed.: *Nicolas Medtner* (London: Dennis Dobson, 1954); pp. 122-32.

Collected Writings from Five Serial Publications, microfilm compiled by Paul Rapoport and Kenneth Derus (unpublished, 1977).

SELECTED WRITINGS BY OTHERS ABOUT SORABJI

"Our music critic": [three reviews of Sorabji performances,] in *The Glasgow Herald*, 2.IV.1930; p. 8—2.XII.1930; p. 6—17.XII.1936; p. 13.

Edmund Rubbra: "Sorabji's enigma", in *The Monthly Musical Record*, vol. 62, Sep. 1932; p. 148.

Edward Clarke Ashworth: "Music—Opus Clavicembalisticum", in *The New English Weekly*, vol. 9 no. 3, 30.IV.1936; p. 55.

[Philip Mairet:] "Valediction to Mr. Sorabji", in *The New English Weekly*, vol. 28 no. 4, 8.XI.1945; p. 34.

Clinton Gray-Fisk: "Kaikhosru Shapurji Sorabji", in *The Musical Times*, no. 1406, vol. 101, Apr. 1960; pp. 230-32.

Erik Chisholm: "Kaikhosru Shapurji Sorabji", privately printed (mid-1960's?) with the preceding and following items.

Frank Holliday: "Splendour upon splendour—on hearing Kaikhosru Shapurji Sorabji play", privately printed (mid-1960's?) with the preceding two items.

Erik Chisholm and Frank Holliday: "The composer Sorabji", transcript of a broadcast talk, privately printed (late 1960's?).

Paul Rapoport: "Sorabji returns?", in *The Musical Times*, no. 1606, vol. 117, Dec. 1976; p. 995.

Hugo Cole: "The ban is off", in *Arts Guardian* of *The Guardian*, 7.XII. 1976; p. 10.

Sacheverell Sitwell: "Kaikhosru Sorabji"—Norman Peterkin: "A note on Kaikhosru Sorabji"—Frank Holliday: "A contribution"—Alistair Hinton: "Kaikhosru Sorabji—an appreciation", in the programme notes to Yonty Solomon's concert in the Wigmore Hall, London, 7. XII.1976; pp. 7-13.

Donald Garvelmann: "Kaikhosru Shapurji Sorabji" [programme notes to Michael Habermann's concert in the Carnegie Recital Hall, New York, 22.V.1977; pp. 1-7].

VIII   Conclusion

Whatever ideas one has for a characterization of *compositionally symphonic* orchestral music, five of the six composers discussed in this book wrote more of it individually than any of the composers usually considered as leading figures who were approximate contemporaries of these five. Consistent, large-scale, hierarchical control of all appropriate musical elements, integration of contrasts, teleological development of musical ideas, and intrinsic dynamism — however vague they sound — are all essential aspects of the independent orchestral works of all five composers. They are important also in much of the work of Schoenberg, Bartók, Stravinsky, and others equally well known. But again, one must generally look beyong the "big names" for the composers who emphasized these matters in large numbers of independent orchestral works, i.e. the composers who returned again and again to symphonic orchestral writing.

This may seem an unimportant assertion, even if accepted, to those who know the history of 20th-century music, for the decline of the symphony orchestra and the decline of compositionally symphonic writing have helped distinguish this history from that of 18th- and 19th-century music.

Yet there is something odd about the statement "Composers don't (or shouldn't) write symphonies any more", which one finds overtly or covertly in many utterances from the past several decades. There obviously *are* composers who do and feel they should write symphonies. It is precisely the *coexistence* of composers who do and those who don't (and think no one should) which is an important distinction of

20th-century music history, as was suggested in Chapter I. If
symphonic composers take a lesser role in an outline history
of 20th-century musical innovation, it is important nonetheless to realize the special nature of that outline and the fact
that symphonic composers represent points of view which are
not extinct. Their music says valid things which other music
may ignore. As Alfred Einstein once put it, "it would be
absurd . . . to reproach someone for continuing to use his legs
since there are motor cars; or for still using motor cars since
he might use a plane."[1] The idea of progress in 20th-century
music is partly a red herring as far as its total history is
concerned.

OPUS EST, from the title of this book, means in Latin not
only *there is artistic achievement*, but also *there is a need*
and *there is a requirement*.

In the face of challenges that it was no longer possible, the
six composers discussed in this book very successfully transformed and renewed aspects of the symphonic tradition (including, in Sorabji's case, the symphonic piano tradition) in
light of 20th-century possibilities and experiences. Vermeulen's ecstatically free polymelodic constructions based on
the new-found essence of the old *cantus-firmus* idea, Holmboe's subtle and profound exploration of techniques and implications of metamorphosis, Brian's wide-ranging and constantly adventuresome treatment of tonality and procedures
of elliptical musical development, Pettersson's devastating
utterances in structures that simultaneously form and collapse, Valen's restless and atonal yet deeply religious and
lyrical counterpoint, Sorabji's demonic intellectual power as
revealed through large-scale control of massive ornamentation
over enormous time spans: all this and very much more makes
the music of all these composers very much worth pursuing,
even for those who, in the most staunchly objective manner,
refuse to admit significance to anything in music but "the
sounds" themselves.

It will be appropriate here to review briefly why the music
of these composers remains relatively unknown. First, there
are general reasons, such as their northern European background and their emphasis (Sorabji excepted) on orchestral

---

[1]   Alfred Einstein: *Greatness in Music*, translated by César Saerchinger (New
York: Oxford University Press, 1941); p. 280.

music, both of which have already been mentioned. The point about orchestral music needs elaboration, however.

It is far more difficult to convince the necessary people to produce performances of unfamiliar or new *orchestral* music than of any other unfamiliar or new music, opera perhaps excepted. Orchestral scores are much harder to grasp quickly on paper than chamber music scores, they involve greater amounts of time, money, and planning to bring to performance, and for this they also depend on a large network of personal and social relations in and around professional symphony orchestra organizations. These organizations are basically not designed to be innovative, but to repeat the standard repertory *ad infinitum*. There are notable exceptions, but without persistent lobbying from living composers and those interested in them, and without the necessary funds from outside agencies, by far most professional orchestras would present much less new music than the small amount they present now. An unknown composer who writes difficult orchestral music will have severe and possibly insurmountable problems getting it played adequately if at all. The situation varies considerably with the country, with the region within any country, and with the background of the composer in question, but regardless of this, it becomes difficult again outside one's own country. Nationalistic economic policies in the arts often make it difficult for large performing organizations to be as interested in foreign contemporary products as they are supposed to be in native ones.

There are also individual reasons why these six composers are not very well known. Many of them have been mentioned in Chapters II to VII. All six composers fought the musical establishment at one time or another, with results for their music roughly predictable according to the strength of their complaints and of the establishment's hold on musical life. The clearest case here is that of Matthijs Vermeulen. As long as Mengelberg controlled Dutch orchestral life, there was no future for Vermeulen or his music in Holland. Vermeulen may also have been ignored later in Holland because of the misunderstood leftist political implications in some of his musical ideas (such as those on the "future orchestra") and nonmusical activities (such as giving an anti-nuclear-weapons speech in 1955 to a crowd of thousands).

All six composers also had personalities which were un-suited to doing the things necessary to get their works per-formed, especially as none of them was really a conductor or had his own orchestra. They were composers first and last, not performers, managers, or salespersons. They wrote the music but only reluctantly could put on the acts needed to entice others to be interested in it. Kaikhosru Sorabji, as could be expected, put the matter in stark relief when he wrote about the necessity for "a plentiful plying of the conductor with his pet booze"[2] and went on to conclude:

> I make bold to say that our composers would be the better for devoting themsleves to   composition alone — and not trying to combine that with the various forms of sycophancy, toadyism and lick-spittling that are the prerequisites to securing perform-ances at the hands of those by whom, in many cases, it were far better never to be performed at all.

The other composers felt they could not afford *not* to try for performances. Despite statements late in his life about never having cared whether his music was played, Havergal Brian did indeed care, and his lack of success in getting it played became a severe financial and psychological difficulty for him for many years.

Various other situations made the music of most of these composers unwanted, situations over which they had no con-trol. The music which Fartein Valen and Allan Pettersson were writing in the 1920's-30's and 1950's-60's respectively was unrelated to current trends in music in their countries. Valen was considered too radical and Pettersson too conser-vative, with similar results. Both Valen and Pettersson also had constant problems with physical illness.

Vagn Holmboe, after winning an important prize for an or-chestral work in 1939, found interest in his bigger works very much reduced during the second world war because of the German occupation of Denmark. The music publisher Viking, which issued Holmboe's music from about 1947 to 1961, went out of business, making many of his works in score or parts now very hard to find.

---

[2]   Kaikhosru Shapurji Sorabji: *Mi Contra Fa—The Immoralisings of a Machia-vellian Musician* (London: Porcupine Press, 1947); p. 147.

It may be argued that other composers faced problems like these and worse and overcame them, becoming deservedly well known. That is true, yet it is still also true that whether these problems are overcome may have nothing to do with the quality or importance of the composer in question. To consider only the two examples of the composers who lived in England: Brian's *Gothic Symphony* remains a brilliant, endlessly fascinating accomplishment despite the fact that it lay unperformed for decades and that the number of people who know it well may still be no more than a dozen, and a similar claim may be made for Sorabji's *Opus Clavicembalisticum*, even though it has not been heard in nearly 50 years and is well known probably by less than half a dozen people. Even if someone thinks *these* claims are wrong, there is nothing illogical in their being applied to unknown works. Yet many people *will* think that this is illogical, because they never admit that anything they do not know about could be worth knowing: if it is unknown, it must be bad, uninteresting, or a cultish craze. Many still hold the belief that music, in its own inevitable and progressive ways, will slowly but surely and automatically bring forth and proclaim its own great works and composers for all to see. Chapter I showed some of the reasons why this belief is wrong: 20th-century music history and contemporary music life both are not what they are often assumed to be. Chapters II to VII did not offer direct proof of Chapter I's assertions, but they did, I hope, offer some valuable evidence. Of course, these six composers are only a few among many symphonic composers who have written challenging, resourceful, original, and profound music that is unlike most 20th-century music currently heard and studied.

This should not be construed as a point awarded to the side of the traditionalists in a contest of them versus the radicals, for there is no need for such a contest, and indeed its existence may really be illusory. Those who think there is a contest are invited to predict an early winner. The others might agree with the possibility that, if there is no solution, then there is no problem. The most traditional and most radical aspects of music just might live together, happily or unhappily ever after, if they are given the chance by all concerned.

APPENDIX I

FORCES REQUIRED IN THE PERFORMANCE OF THE WORKS DISCUSSED IN DETAIL IN CHAPTERS II TO VI

Note: Doublings are indicated for the winds but not for the percussion.

Matthijs Vermeulen: SYMPHONY NO. 2, *Prélude à la Nouvelle Journée*

4	flutes (4 piccolos)	tympani (4 players)
4	oboes (2 English horns)	side drum
2	E^b clarinets (1 clarinet)	tenor drum
3	clarinets	bass drum
1	bass clarinet	castanets
3	bassoons	tamtam
1	contrabassoon	xylophone
4	horns	2 harps
2	E^b trumpets	
4	trumpets	strings
3	tenor trombones	
1	tuba	

Note: In one passage the score calls for four tympanists, but two could
      manage it.

Vagn Holmboe: SYMPHONY NO. 7

1	piccolo	tympani
2	flutes	side drum
2	oboes (1 English horn)	tenor drum
2	clarinets	bass drum
2	bassoons	cymbals
		triangle
4	horns	xylophone
3	trumpets	celesta
3	trombones	
1	tuba	strings

Havergal Brian: SYMPHONY NO. 1, *The Gothic*

Part I

2 piccolos (1 flute)	tympani (2 players)
3 flutes (1 alto flute)	side drum
2 oboes	2 bass drums
1 oboe d'amore	cymbals
1 English horn	triangle
1 bass oboe	tambourine
1 E^b clarinet	gong
2 clarinets	glockenspiel
1 basset horn	xylophone
1 bass clarinet	celesta
3 bassoons	organ
1 contrabassoon	
	2 harps
6 horns	
1 E^b cornet	strings
4 trumpets	
3 tenor trombones	
2 tubas	

Part II

2 piccolos (1 flute)	tympani (2 players)
6 flutes (1 alto flute)	2 side drums
6 oboes (1 oboe d'amore, 1 bass oboe)	2 bass drums
	long drum
2 English horns	cymbals (6 players)
2 E^b clarinets (1 clarinet)	2 triangles
4 clarinets	2 tambourines
2 basset horns	gong
2 bass clarinets	thunder machine
1 contrabass clarinet	chains
3 bassoons	bird scare
2 contrabassoons	glockenspiel
	xylophone
8 horns	chimes
2 E^b cornets	tubular bells
8 trumpets	celesta
1 bass trumpet	organ
3 tenor trombones	
1 bass trombone (1 contrabass trombone)	2 harps
1 contrabass trombone	strings
2 euphoniums	
2 tubas	

plus 4 brass bands, each containing 2 horns, 2 trumpets, 2 tenor trom-
bones, 2 tubas, and tympani (1 player); and 4 vocal soloists (SATB),
2 double choruses, and children's chorus.

Notes: 1. It is possible to reduce the instrumentation slightly.
         2. The long drum and thunder machine are not found in the
            published score but were required by Brian. It is possible
            that they are found in the final full score autograph manu-
            script, which has been missing for many years.

Allan Pettersson: SYMPHONY NO. 2

2 flutes (2 piccolos)	tympani
2 oboes	side drum
2 clarinets (1 bass clarinet)	tenor drum
2 bassoons	bass drum
	cymbals
2 horns	tamtam
2 trumpets	xylophone
2 trombones	celesta
	strings

Fartein Valen: SONETTO DI MICHELANGELO

2 flutes	1 horn
2 oboes	
2 clarinets	strings
2 bassoons	

NENIA

2 flutes	1 horn
2 oboes	1 trumpet
2 clarinets	
2 bassoons	strings

CANTICO DI RINGRAZIAMENTO

2 flutes	2 horns	cymbals
2 oboes	2 trumpets	
2 clarinets	1 bass trombone	strings
2 bassoons		

AN DIE HOFFNUNG

2 flutes	1 horn	harp (or celesta or piano)
2 oboes	1 trumpet	
2 clarinets		
2 bassoons		strings